grade study-mate

H. Leitch and N. McGhee

- **a handbook of practical advice and practice questions**

french

Hamilton Publishing

standard grade study-mate

french

First published 1996
© H. Leitch and N. McGhee 1996

ISBN 0 946164 29 0

A catalogue record for this book is available from the British Library.

Orders can be made *direct* over the phone
Contact Thomson Litho, Hamilton Publishing (Sales)
on (01335) 233081

Access and Visa Cards accepted

Letter accepted with school or personal cheque

Published by
Hamilton Publishing
A division of M & A Thomson Litho Limited
10–16 Colvilles Place, Kelvin Industrial Estate,
East Kilbride G75 0SN

Printed and bound in Great Britain by
M & A Thomson Litho Ltd., East Kilbride, Scotland

Contents

Acknowledgements

The authors wish to thank all colleagues who gave help and advice — in particular Ian Boffey, Jean Nisbet, Anne Welsh and May Winton. Thanks also to the pupils who volunteered to try out the material.

The authors and publisher would like to thank the following for giving their permission to reproduce copyright material on the pages listed.

Extracts

Ministère de l'Agriculture et de la Pêche, page 2; *France-Soir*/Société Presse-Alliance, pages 10, 14, 23 and 38; Les Bateaux Parisiens, page 11; Les Cinés Gaumont, page 12; Librairie Gründ, page 14; United Feature Syndicate Inc, page 15; *Okapi*/Bayard Presse, pages 15, 16, 21, 26, 27, 29, 32, 39, 42, 82, 84, 85, 86, 88 and 89; P & T Productions SPRL, page 17; L'École des Loisirs, pages 19 and 20; Glénat Editions, page 27; Les Editions Mondon MBM, page 40; *Phosphore*/Bayard Presse, pages 41 and 50; Abedition, page 52; HarperCollins Publishers Ltd, pages 71 and 97.

The authors and publisher have made every attempt to contact copyright holders. They apologise for any unwitting infringement of copyright.

Photographs

Les Bateaux Parisiens, page 11; Les Cinés Gaumont, page 12; Worldvision Enterprise Corporation, page 22; Robert P. Comport/Animals Animals/ Oxford Scientific Films, page 24; Michael and Patricia Fogden, page 25; Stills Press, pages 26 and 51; Warner Brothers, page 29; Tristar Pictures, page 32; Rodney Mullen/Action Plus, page 41; Gamma Press, page 42; Simone Wallich/J'étais une fois/Société d'Editions, page 46; Age Concern, page 48.

Introduction

This *Study-Mate* has been written to help you develop the skills of reading French with understanding, of speaking French with confidence and of writing French relevantly and accurately. This is, in the first instance, to help you to do well in your Standard Grade exams, but it is also to give you the satisfaction of being able to read, speak and write French well, and to give you a sound basis for further development in the language, whether in further study in school or university, or for use in future employment.

The tests included are based on those currently used in the Standard Grade examinations. The format of exam papers can be checked by looking at sample papers. Here, the questions have been arranged for the style of the *Study-Mate*, so do not be put off in your exam if the questions *look* slightly different. From time to time the arrangements for the testing of languages may be altered (for example one skill may be considered more or less important than the others, or the way the answers are marked may change). Your teacher should inform you in plenty of time of the exact requirements. However, the skills you develop through working with this book should be useful to you, no matter how they are tested.

It would be wise to begin your preparation for the examinations well in advance to give yourself time to develop the skills you will need to use. It is not possible to do well in Standard Grade French by swotting furiously for the last few weeks before the exams. So give some thought as to how you can use this book, along with your class work, when planning your studies. It is probably best to set aside a certain time each week when you will include some practice from *Study-Mate French* along with your normal homework.

Use your commonsense in selecting the sections which are most relevant to your needs. If you and your teacher feel that you should be aiming to do well in the Credit paper, do not spend too much time on the sections that deal with General Level. On the other hand, if you and your teacher feel that you are likely to get a General Award, those are the sections on which you should concentrate. If you are somewhere in between — or if you do not know where you are — start at General and then push yourself a little to tackle some of the Credit tasks.

You may feel that you wish to develop one skill rather than all those which are dealt with here. By all means, concentrate on the area in which you feel you need most help, but you should not neglect completely the other skills, as they all contribute to building up your language resources.

Each chapter explains clearly what you will find in that section of the exam paper and gives you advice on how to direct your performance with several tasks to help you improve. In Chapter Seven you will find further help with the General and Credit reading passages and in Chapter Eight there are suggested answers to the tasks.

The most important part of any book is *you*, the reader. It is *your* effort which will determine how well you improve your command of French. *Your* efforts will be rewarded not only by a good exam grade but also by the ability to understand and communicate with people from all over the world.

Courage et bonne chance!

HL and NMcG, 1996

CHAPTER ONE

Understanding French

In the Standard Grade examination you will have to show that you understand written and spoken French. Using the techniques in this book will help you improve your performance and your grades by making sure that you tackle the tasks set in the best possible way. You should use the techniques described when practising in class and at home so that you do them automatically in the exam.

READING

In this and the following two chapters you should practise six steps to help you read more effectively.

REMEMBER

Use your time wisely.	*Read the question carefully.*
Think ahead.	*Select the information you need.*
Use your dictionary with care.	*Check your answers.*

Use Your Time Wisely

It is important that you use your time sensibly in the exam. In the General paper you will have to complete between *five* long and *eight* short sections in 45 minutes. So you must complete each part in 5 to 10 minutes. You will not gain any marks for sections or questions which you do not attempt because you run out of time. At Credit level you must read *three* to *five* quite long sections in an hour — that is about 15 minutes for each passage.

You should not spend exactly the same amount of time on each section. The number of marks allocated to each question and to each section will vary. Spending a few minutes glancing through the paper to see how the marks are distributed will help you decide how much time you can spend on each part. Do not waste your time struggling with a question worth only 1 mark when you might pick up 4 marks elsewhere.

You do not have to work through the paper in the order in which it is set out. If a first glance suggests one passage is easier than the others, begin with that one, then return to the rest. Similarly, when you try the reading passages in this book, pick those which *you* find easiest first.

It will take you longer to finish the practice exercises in this book than it will in the exam or even one you would do in class, as you have to read the instructions as well as answering the questions. With practice, however, you will learn to read passages more quickly. At the end of the chapters on General Reading and Credit Reading you will find practice test papers so that when you sit the Standard Grade exam you will feel confident about the way you are going to answer the questions.

Think Ahead

Each reading passage in the exam is introduced by a **heading** which is *not* in French. In their excitement, many candidates forget to read this introduction. But the heading is there to help you. By reading it first you will have a rough idea of what the passage is about. So, it will help to prevent you panicking because there are words you may not have seen before. Knowing roughly what the passage is about should help you to guess intelligently and should also stop you writing ridiculous answers.

The **questions** which follow the passages will also make the meaning of the passage clearer and *you should read them before you read the text.*

Here is an example of how the heading and questions in the exam paper can help you.

▶ First read the introductory **heading**. This might say:
You pick up a leaflet about preventing forest fires.

▶ Now read the **questions**:
(a) Where are you not allowed to light a fire?
(b) What else can you do to prevent fires?

Both the heading and the questions make it clear that the text will be about forest fires. What kind of words will you expect to find in the passage? Here are some suggestions: fire; forest; matches; to light; cigarettes.

Think about any other ideas you may have just now before we look at the passage in more detail. You will probably not find all of these words but you will have a general idea of what you can expect before you read the passage itself. Predicting the kind of vocabulary you can expect will help you avoid using the dictionary too often, and save time for finding the answers to the questions.

Use Your Dictionary With Care

You are allowed to use a *dictionary* to help you find meanings in the exam but remember that you will not have time to look up every word. Learning to anticipate and guess the sense will save time for the words you need to find. Try the exercises in this book without using your dictionary unless absolutely necessary.

If this is your own book, begin by underlining (in pencil) the words in the passage which you know already. This will focus your attention on the general sense of the text which you can bear in mind while you read the questions.

If it is not your book, check with your teacher that underlining in pencil is allowed.

Look now at the following extract from a pamphlet on forest fires and underline or note all the words which you can understand or can guess.

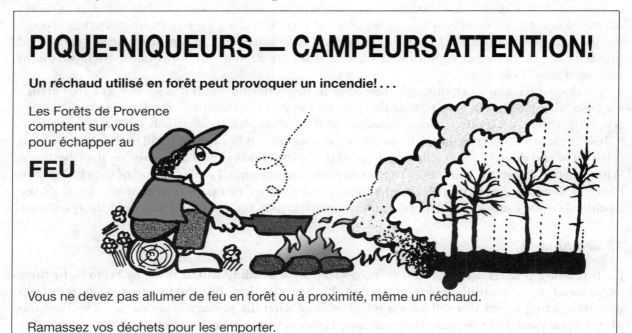

PIQUE-NIQUEURS — CAMPEURS ATTENTION!

Un réchaud utilisé en forêt peut provoquer un incendie!...

Les Forêts de Provence
comptent sur vous
pour échapper au

FEU

Vous ne devez pas allumer de feu en forêt ou à proximité, même un réchaud.

Ramassez vos déchets pour les emporter.

Laissez la forêt propre.

© Ministère de l'Agriculture et de la Pêche, 1995

There may still be a few words which you do not understand and which you think will make the sense of the text clearer. But . . . before you reach for a dictionary, there are several tricks which may help you work out the meaning. You will find tips on how to do this with several of the practice passages.

Read the passage about forest fires again. Here are some clues to help you work out some of the meanings. This time underline or note:

(a) at least four words which look like English words.

(b) a word where you can substitute an 's' for a circumflex (ˆ), so that the word looks like an English word.

(c) a word where you can add an 's' after 'é', to make a word like an English word.

(d) two words which look like French words you already know.

You can check the words you found in this passage in Chapter Seven 'Hints for Reading Passages'. Use this chapter carefully. It will be useful if you are finding a particular task difficult. But don't be tempted to turn to Chapter Seven too quickly. Remember that the more you improve your technique the easier you will find the examination.

Dictionaries are normally supplied for classwork and for the exams but we would strongly advise you to buy one of your own. School dictionaries are sometimes vandalised, lost or they disappear. If you can take care of your own, then you will know it is in good condition for the exam. It will be useful for homework. By using the same one regularly you can get used to the feel of it and be able to find your way around it more quickly. By buying your own dictionary you will be able to choose one that you like. You will find advice on how to choose a dictionary on page 116.

Read The Question Carefully

The questions you will be asked may involve:

— saying whether statements about the passage are true or false;

— completing a grid with information from the passage;

— saying which of two items like magazines or hotels appeals more to you and why.

Most commonly the questions ask directly what you have understood about the text — Who? What? Where? When? Why? It may seem obvious to stress that you must answer the question you have been asked, but some candidates just write down all the information they understand in the passage and hope for the best. The marks given for each question will indicate how much detail you must give. Some of the General Level papers have spaces in which the answers are to be written. The number of lines in these spaces is another indication of the number of points of information sought.

Look more carefully at the questions about forest fires.

QUESTIONS

Marks

(a) Where are you not allowed to light a fire? (2)

- There are *two* marks for this question and it asks 'where' so your answer will give **two places**.

TIP   Look for prepositions to fix places — like dans, à, en, près de.

(b) What else can you do to prevent fires? (3)

- This time there are *three* marks, and you are asked what you can **do**, so you will be looking for **verbs**. Look out for anything you are told not to do.

TIP   Verbs which give formal instructions in French often end in -ez. In the dictionary you will find them ending in -er, -re or -ir.

Select The Information You Need

Now read the passage again and circle or use a wavy line to underline the phrases you will need in your answers. Write down your answers **in English** — not in French — using your dictionary now, if necessary, to check for meanings. Remember that you do not need to write your answers in full sentences as long as you make your meaning clear.

You can check your answers to the reading passages in Chapter Eight. Again, don't be tempted to turn to it until you are sure you have written down as much as you can on your own. For some of the practice texts like this one, you will find hints in Chapter Seven to help you find the answers if you find the task difficult.

Check Your Answers

Leave at least **five minutes** at the end of the exam to read through the whole paper and check your answers. It is so easy to misspell or miss out a word you meant to include. You may describe someone as 'spoty', then the examiner must guess if you meant 'spotty' or 'sporty'. If you miss out 'not', it can change the whole meaning of your answer.

If you can work with a friend while you are preparing for the exam, begin by taking turns to check each other's answers. This will help train your eye for the kind of words or phrases which are easily omitted.

Try to write an answer for each question — an intelligent guess may gain you a mark or two where a blank will certainly not. If you have to make up an answer, remember to bear in mind the theme of the passage.

A WORD ABOUT LISTENING

This chapter has referred mostly to techniques for reading and you will find more passages, with help and without, in the next two chapters. It is obviously not possible to include similar practice questions for listening in a book, but you should use every opportunity to practise listening to French.

In addition to the practice you will have in the classroom, you can improve your listening *and* relax by watching some of the many French films which are now shown on television and in the cinemas. Try experimenting with your radio in the evenings to find a French station. It is fun to guess from the tone of voice, without even listening to the words, whether you are listening to a football commentary, a news report or an advert. When you listen in class and in the exam to the way the people speak, it will give you a clue as to the meaning. Do they sound happy or sad, impatient or resigned?

If your school allows you to borrow cassettes to practise at home, try to set aside a regular time each week to do this. If you have a French pen-friend, why not suggest exchanging cassettes as well as letters?

If you find it difficult to concentrate on a tape, try listening to some speech programmes in English on the radio and note down the details of what you hear.

If you have any hearing problems, make sure your school is aware of this well in advance of the exam. They will be able to make special arrangements for you.

TECHNIQUE

Like reading, listening is worth 25% of the total marks at Standard Grade. The length of the extract may vary from one short sentence to longer passages of seven to nine sentences in the Credit paper. As the passages get longer, there may be more than one question on each section and you may also be expected to give more details in your answer. Words like *d'abord* (firstly), *deuxièmement* (secondly) and such like are sometimes used to give you a clue to each point which is being made.

You are commonly asked, especially at General Level, about the weather, to describe people and objects and where and when events happened. You must also be able to say what happened. For this you will need to recognise most verbs in the past tense.

Many of the techniques which you will use for reading will also apply to listening, although you are not allowed to use a dictionary.

The timing of each question is controlled by the tape-recorder. You will hear each section twice and again reading the heading and the questions first will help you think ahead. There will be a short pause between the two readings and a longer pause to allow you to write your answer before you hear the next section. Do not write your answers until you have heard the tape twice. You may miss some information if you are writing while the tape is playing.

Your final answer must be in English but if you hear a word and you cannot remember what it means, jot it down in French. Don't worry about the spelling here, you can score out the French word and write down the proper translated form, if you remember it, at the end of the exam.

You have **five minutes** at the end of the exam to check your answers. Have you included all the information you meant to? Look again at the number of marks for each question. Can you add anything from your rough notes in French? Have you left any blanks? If so, make an intelligent guess now.

REMEMBER

Think ahead.
Read the question carefully.
Make rough notes in French if you have to (but score them out at the end).

Listen — then write.
Check your answers.
Leave no blanks.

CHAPTER TWO

General Reading

How are you reading this book? Did you start at Chapter One to read through to the end? Or did you look at the Contents page to decide which parts of the exam you need to practise, selecting the most important parts for you, and only glancing at the rest to make sure you have not missed anything?

Whatever you read, in any language, you will use several different techniques. The first method is probably how you read a novel. The second is the way you read a textbook or work of reference. In other words, you adapt your reading to the text and to the purpose of your reading.

Think of how you read a magazine. Before you buy the magazine you may quickly read the contents or flick through the pages to see which articles might interest you. This is called **skimming** — getting an overall impression of what a text is about. Then you see an article about a new television programme starring your favourite actor or actress. You ignore the rest and turn to the part which tells you when it is going to be on. This is called **scanning** — looking through a passage for particular pieces of information. If you want to read a short story, you will want to take more time, reading from the beginning to the end. As you read you will have an impression of the characters, not only from what you are told directly but also from what they say and do. This is **close reading** of the text — reading 'between the lines', interpreting the underlying meaning of the text.

While you automatically use all three methods when reading your own language, you must also practise them when reading French both in class and in the exam. You will improve the speed at which you read and thus improve your performance. You will also increase your enjoyment of reading the foreign language — any text will become boring if you are trying to read it by looking up every word in a dictionary.

SKIMMING

As we said in Chapter One, reading the heading and the questions first (which are not in French) on each passage will help you predict what kind of vocabulary you can expect in your question. Skimming through the text will also help you to understand the gist of the meaning and help you focus on the kind of information you are given. Remember this should be a very quick reading, but, as you read, underline in pencil or note one or two words which you understand or can guess. This will help you concentrate on the general sense of the passage.

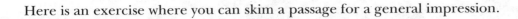

Here is an exercise where you can skim a passage for a general impression.

A. Vous avez des brûlures d'estomac? Des sensations d'aigreurs et de pesanteur? Ces désagréments sont dus à une sécrétion d'acide provoquée par des substances irritantes (épices, graisses cuites, alcool, café, tabac) ou par le stress. Pour les soulager, voici un remède végétal. . .

B. En sortant du bain, offrez à vos pieds une rapide mise en beauté. Comme pour les mains, repoussez les cuticules. Éliminez ensuite les callosités à l'aide d'une râpe spécifique (Scholl). . .

C. J'ai 13 ans et une petite sœur de 5 ans. Depuis que mes parents sont séparés, je ne m'entends plus avec ma mère. . . Je ne sais plus que faire. . . Donnez-moi un conseil, je vous en prie. Et si les filles de mon âge ont le même problème, qu'elles vous écrivent à vous et vous me ferez suivre le courrier.

D. Gaëlle n'avait pas imaginé l'homme d'affaires si jeune, avec cette allure sportive et ce regard d'un bleu intense. Elle se sentit fondre et lutta de toutes ses forces contre l'étrange faiblesse qui la gagnait. . .

E. Battre 4 oeufs en omelette, puis ajouter 250 g de crème fraîche, 2 c à café de farine et 200 g de crabe en bâtons, coupé en petits morceaux. Ajouter 1 pincée de paprika, saler et poivrer. . .

F. A posséder dans sa garde-robe: un manteau en laine mélangée (La Redoute, 790 F), sur un twin-set en maille multicolore (Galeries Lafayette, 670 F et 450 F) et un short en flanelle à pinces et revers (Burton, 269 F).

© *Maxi*, 28 decembre 1992

REMEMBER

Use your time wisely.	*Read the question carefully.*
Think ahead.	*Select the information you need.*
Use your dictionary with care.	*Check your answers.*

Which of the previous articles (A, B, C, D, E or F) would you expect to find in a magazine under these headings?

1. Cookery	4. Health	*Marks*
2. Fashion	5. Story	
3. Beauty	6. Problem page	(6)

TIP Begin with the questions which seem easiest first (in this case possibly the cookery page), then do the rest.

If you find this really difficult, look at Chapter Seven. If you find it too easy turn to Chapter Three 'Credit Reading'.

SCANNING

When you read a text for particular information, you will read it more slowly and more carefully than in your first glance through. But you do not need to understand every word as you read. The skill here is to know what information to ignore. This time bear in mind the questions to which you are looking for answers. As you read, pencil in (if you are allowed to) — by drawing a circle or box round — any **key phrases** which you think contain the information you need.

Look at this example.
In a magazine you see this photo and the article which goes with it. You wonder what it is about.

Drap de plage pour chiens ou chats

Dans la lignée des Japonais qui offrent des séjours luxueux dans des grands hôtels à leur chien ou à leur chat, ne partez pas à la plage sans emporter ce confortable drap de bain avec capote rabattable pour qu'il ne souffre pas d'un excès de chaleur.

© *VSD*, 9/15 juillet 1992

QUESTIONS

Marks

(a) For whom or what has this beach lounger been designed? (1)
 • Read the whole text several times to find the answer. Don't pick out the first word which catches your eye. There may be information elsewhere in the passage.

(b) What feature makes it especially useful? (1)
 • The photos and drawings which accompany the text will also give you a general idea of what it is about but don't rely on them for detailed information.

(c) Why would it be useful? (2)
 • The key phrase which introduces the answer here is *pour qu(e)*. You will know *pour* meaning 'for' as a preposition. If you look under all the entries for *pour* in the dictionary you will find what it means as a conjunction; *souffre* and *excès* will remind you of English words.

Sometimes you will be asked to find specific information so that you can compare two articles. Here the question may not be as helpful. It will probably be something vague like 'Which of these would you prefer?'

 The technique however is the same as you use to scan any other passage. Find the words you know first, then underline in pencil or highlight the key phrases. If you are to compare the passages ignore those features which they have in common and concentrate on the differences.

 Do not be tempted to write 'I would not choose either of them'. This does not tell the examiner that you have understood the French. Remember too that the examiner does not know you personally and so does not know which you would prefer. You are not being asked to make a real choice, but to show that you can understand the differences. Choose the one you can understand best. In real life you will have more time to reach a decision.

You are trying to decide which of these campsites to choose. The prices are about the same.

CAMPING CARAVANNING ✩✩✩✩
L'Etoile d'Argens

☐ CALME

☐ CONFORT

☐ RIVIÈRE

Emplacements délimités de 100 m² avec branchements électriques — eau.

À 2 km de la mer — Embarcadère fluvial — Pêche — Canotage — Pédalos — Terrain de jeux — Épicerie — Piscine

PÂQUES A LA FIN SEPTEMBRE — TÉLÉPHONE 44.23.00

© St Aygulf Syndicat d'Initiative

La Résidence du Campeur
✩ ✩ ✩ ✩

Emplacements délimités de 100 m² — Électricité — Eau chaude
Accès direct à la plage par souterrain

SANITAIRES INDIVIDUELS

Plats à emporter — Calme — Confort — Gardé et éclairé toute la nuit
Tennis — Jeux de plage — Parasols
Initiation à la plongée et à la pêche sous-marine

OUVERT TOUTE L'ANNÉE

Téléphone 44.26.37

© St Aygulf Syndicat d'Initiative

QUESTION

Marks

Which would you prefer? (Give **two** reasons.)

(2)

9

CLOSE READING

Occasionally at General Level, and more often at Credit Level, you will be asked to interpret the facts in the passage. You will not be able to lift the answers straight from the text. The answers will be there, of course, but you will need to read it more carefully to find the information you require. This will take more time than purely factual questions and this is where you will benefit from reading the easier passages more quickly. Begin by checking in your own mind that you have understood the general sense of the passage. Then use your dictionary to understand any sections which are still not clear. When you write your answers *first* state your general conclusion *then* give evidence from the passage to back up your answer.

> **TIP** Include all the relevant information which you can understand. Check the marks to see if you have covered all the points needed. But do not translate large sections of the text. You will be wasting time and may lose marks if you misunderstand part of the meaning and write down contradictory statements.

You notice this article in the newspaper.

Avion disparu: on cherche

© *France-Soir*, 24 juin 1993

Les recherches se poursuivaient, mercredi en fin d'après-midi, dans le Haut-Rhin pour retrouver un avion de tourisme monomoteur qui a disparu, mardi soir, alors qu'il survolait la région. L'appareil effectuait une liaison Berne-Luxembourg avec seulement le pilote à bord. Les recherches se sont concentrées dans un secteur montagneux et boisé des Vosges, près des villages de Dellering et Moosch.

QUESTIONS
Marks

(a) When did the aeroplane disappear? (1)
- The answer to the first question is quite straightforward. Two days are mentioned but only one refers directly to the disappearance of the aeroplane. You will be able to find the word for disappeared if you do not already know it as it looks very like the English word.

(b) Why might the search be difficult? (2)
- To find the answer to the second question you will have to have a clear idea of the whole story. There is no part in the text beginning 'The search will be difficult because. . .'. You will have noticed that you **are** given information about
  - — *when the incident happened*
  - — *what kind of plane it was*
  - — *what the plane was doing*
  - — *where the incident took place.*
- Which of these is likely to affect the difficulty of the search? This is where you have to use your commonsense to find the answer. As a further clue look at the parts of the text which tell you about the search. You know the verb 'chercher' to look for. Can you find a noun with the same root?

Here are some further examples where you can practise your reading technique. Don't worry too much just now about timing. That will be easier the more experience you have.

> **TIP** Every time you look a word up in the dictionary make a small pencil mark in the margin. If you have looked a word up three times it's time to learn it by heart.

You and your family are on holiday in Paris. You decide to take a boat trip on the River Seine. Your parents have picked up a leaflet and ask you to tell them the details.

DÉCOUVREZ PARIS AVEC LES PLUS PARISIENS DES BATEAUX

Toute l'année, la traversée complète de Paris à bord de nos bateaux entièrement vitrés, offrant une vision panoramique. Une heure de croisière, les ponts et monuments de Paris commentés par nos hôtesses.

Départ toutes les trente minutes; le soir, croisière des illuminations.

HORAIRE: De 9 h 30 à 22 h 30

PRIX: Adultes, 30 F, Enfants de moins de 12 ans, 15 F

DEPART: Pont d'Iena, rive gauche au pied de la Tour Eiffel.

METRO: TROCADERO & BIR-HAKEIM.
RER: CHAMPS-DE-MARS.
BUS: 42, 69, 82

© Les Bateaux Parisiens, Paris

QUESTIONS   *Marks*

(a) How often do the boats leave?   (1)
(b) How long does the trip last?   (1)
•   Both these questions ask about **times**. Note or underline any time phrases you can find in the text.

> **TIP**   You will frequently want to know when and how often events take place, not only in the exam but also when you visit France. Check now that you can recognise the main time phrases: days of the week, months, seasons and dates.

To give a precise answer you must pay attention to phrases like:
(i)   matin, après-midi, soir
(ii)   durée, pendant
(iii) (à partir) du, (jusqu') à
(iv)   tous les/toutes les
(v)   sauf.

Can you match the phrases with these meanings?
1. every
2. during
3. from, till
4. except
5. morning, afternoon, evening

Add and learn any new phrases you meet more than once.

(c) How much does it cost?   (2)
•   Note or underline any prices in the text. You must make it clear to whom the prices apply. Are there any age limits?

(d) Where do you get the boat?   (2)
•   You will know that 'Départ' indicates where you will find the information in the text and recognise 'Pont d'Iena' and 'la Tour Eiffel'. There is no real English equivalent of 'Pont d'Iena' so you can quote this from the text. But we do have an English expression for 'la Tour Eiffel', so put this into your own words. Giving these two place names will not be enough to show you understand the French. Find two phrases which give you more exact information.

(e) How can you get there?   (3)
•   There will be no problem finding three means of transport, but you may have to explain one where there is no exact counterpart in English.

You notice this article about cinema prices in the newspaper.

Les cinés Gaumont cassent les prix

32 francs !
Tout compte fait
c'est bien d'être petit.

dans les cinémas Gaumont
si tu as moins de 12 ans, c'est 32 francs
tout le temps.

Depuis le 16 novembre, l'entrée dans tous les cinémas Gaumont est fixée à 32 F pour les moins de 12 ans, tous les jours et à n'importe quelle heure. Profitez-en, ou pensez à en faire profiter petits frères et petites soeurs.
    Vous n'avez plus aucune excuse pour ne pas les emmener au ciné!

© Les cinés Gaumont

QUESTIONS

Marks

(a) What is the special offer from Gaumont cinemas?   (1)
  • Where there is a headline to an article it often sums up what the article is about. Notice that 'casser' cannot be translated by its literal meaning 'to break'. Can you think of a better way to express this in English? Check the text to see what further details it gives you of the offer.

(b) When is the offer valid?   (3)
  • Part of the answer here is very easy as you can quickly find the date in the text. But is it **on**, **from** or **until** that date?

> **TIP**   Make sure you write down your answer in English — the French word looks so like the English one, it would be easy to make a mistake. Remember, all your answers must be in English.

  • There are three parts to question (b). Look again at the text.

(c) Which age group can take advantage of it?   (1)
  • Again it is easy to find an age mentioned in the text but is it **for** this age group or those who are **under** or those who are **over**?

(d) If you do not qualify for this offer, how else does the article suggest you can use it?   (1)
  • Look for a word which in English could mean 'to take advantage of'.

You pick up a magazine and notice an advert for activity holidays for young people.

Vacances avec les Copains
(6 à 12 ans)

Voile, mini-golf, baignade, camping...

A 12 km au nord de la Baule, réparti sur un terrain de près de 2,5 hectares qui jouxte la mer, le centre est composé de quatre bâtiments. Hébergement en chambres de six lits avec les sanitaires attenants. Salle à manger, éclairée par de grandes baies vitrées, qui domine la mer. Grandes salles d'activités, salle de ping-pong, et salon bibliothèque.

Les activités dominantes sont celles qui se pratiquent en bord de mer: voile, mini-golf, baignade, pêche et découverte de la région à travers les campings.

Attention: un brevet de 50 m de natation est nécessaire pour la pratique de la voile.

© Vacances Gentilly

QUESTIONS

Marks

(a) What sleeping accommodation is offered? (2)
* You will immediately recognise the word 'chambre' for a bedroom but this will obviously not be enough for two marks. You must also describe the rooms.

(b) What facilities are there on the site for leisure? (3)
* You are being asked about what is available, **not** what you can do. If you look ahead you will see that question (d) asks about what you can do. You cannot give the same answer to two questions.

(c) What do you require to take part in sailing? (2)
* Again you are being asked about a 'thing' not what you should be able to do. So you are looking for a noun not a verb. 'What you require' = 'what is necessary'. Find a French word like 'necessary' which will point you to the correct part of the text.

(d) Apart from sailing, name two other outdoor activities which are offered. (2)
* Notice the wording of this question. Clearly there will not be a mark for 'sailing' as it is given in the question. You are asked for **two** activities. Pick two which you understand easily (i.e. without the dictionary) if possible. Do not write any more than two. You will not gain any more marks and may lose some if you are inaccurate.

You notice this article in the news section of the paper.

Serpents cachés

Un Taïwannais a été condamné mercredi aux Etats-Unis à une peine de prison pour trafic de reptiles. Il avait été arrêté à l'aéroport international de Los Angeles où il s'apprêtait à prendre l'avion. Il dissimulait 18 serpents enroulés autour de ses biceps et de ses chevilles. En tout, les policiers ont saisi 52 serpents achetés en Californie et que le trafiquant voulait exporter illégalement à Taïwan.

© *France-Soir*, 3 septembre 1993

QUESTIONS   *Marks*

(a) Where exactly was the man arrested?   (1)
  * Notice the wording of the question. It asks you to be **exact** in your answer. Giving the name of the country will not be enough. Underline or note all the places mentioned in the text.

(b) Why was he sent to prison?   (1)
  * The headline will give you a general idea of the theme of the passage and you will find more details in the text. Be careful not to jump to conclusions here, though. The word 'serpent' is a *faux ami* (false friend); that is, it does not mean the same as the English word it looks like. Think about it! Another key word here is 'illégalement'. Remember that words ending in **-ment** in French often end in **-ly** in English. Try saying the word out loud.

(c) How was he trying to do this? Give details.   (2)
  * Here you are asked to give a detailed answer. Notice that the verbs in this passage are written in the past tenses. Remember a dictionary will only give the infinitive of verbs.

> **TIP** In order to retell a story you must be able to recognise these common endings:
> -é,-i, -u indicate a completed action (= -(e)d, -(e)t or -(e)n in English).

In a magazine you notice this puzzle.

Devinette

Une grosse tête, un long cou, quelques dents
Qui brillent comme de l'argent,
Ce petit personnage
Ouvre tous les passages
Et, pour entrer dans la maison,
Il faut sa permission.

From *Devinettes et Mystères en Couleurs*, 1991 © Librairie Gründ, Paris

QUESTION   *Marks*

What do you think the puzzle is about, A, B, C or D?

A   giraffe
B   comb
C   key
D   door   (1)

  * At first sight this may seem an easy question as you will recognise most of the words from class work but all of the suggested answers have some of the features described in the poem. Only one has them all. You will need to understand the whole text to make the correct choice. You must read the question and the puzzle several times to get the answer.

You will need to read the text very carefully when you are asked to **explain** the meaning of a text.

Make sure first that you understand what is happening or has happened. Then try putting it into your own words as though you were telling it to a friend, not just translating the French. Finally write down your answer.

To practise, find a member of your family or a friend who does not speak French and tell them about this cartoon. If they do not understand your explanation, there will be points which you must clarify.

Your young brother is a Snoopy fan. He asks you to explain this cartoon.

PEANUTS ● Par Schulz

© 1992 United Feature Syndicate Inc.

QUESTION

Marks

Why is Marcy disappointed in her marks?   (2)

There are no tips or hints for the remaining passages in this chapter. Concentrate on developing your technique by reading each passage several times — for the general sense and then for particular information. Try to limit the number of times you use a dictionary by thinking ahead to the kind of information you will be given.

Keep a note of how long it takes you to find as many answers as you can — but no more than five to ten minutes on average — for each passage.

Remember to check over your answers before you look at the marking scheme in Chapter Eight.

The first three texts are taken from an article with some good advice on how to improve your memory. You may have noticed by now that many of the passages are about 50 words in length. You may want to read longer texts in class and at home and it is a good idea to break them into smaller sections if you find the whole article too intimidating.

Étonnez votre mémoire!

La matière grise déteste surtout l'ennui et la monotonie. Vous retiendrez plus vite si vous jouez toute la journée avec votre mémoire. Le matin, en route vers le collège, posez-vous des questions. Quels objets avez-vous vus en passant devant telle vitrine? Combien de grands bruns moustachus aperçus aujourd'hui?

Adapted from *Okapi*,
15–28 février 1993

QUESTIONS

Marks

(a) According to the article, why should you play memory games?   (2)

(b) Give an example of the kind of question you could practise on the way to school.   (1)

Chaque jour privilégiez un sens. Regardez, le lundi, tout ce qui est jaune. Le soir, dressez une liste! Le mercredi, consacrez-vous aux odeurs. En les énumérant, plus tard, classez-les en bonnes et mauvaises. Le vendredi, imaginez que la police vous interroge au sujet d'un crime: «Que faisiez-vous samedi dernier à 18 h 00?» Sans alibi, vous devenez un suspect. Alors, accrochez-vous!

Adapted from *Okapi*,
15–28 février 1993

QUESTIONS

Marks

(a) Which three of the following is it suggested you encourage?   (3)
   A   Hearing
   B   Imagination
   C   Sight
   D   Smell
   E   Taste
   F   Touch

(b) Choose any **one** of the senses mentioned in the text and explain exactly how you can develop it.   (2)

Accordez des récréations à votre mémoire. Elle ne peut pas fonctionner 24 heures sur 24. Travaillez pendant un maximum de vingt à quarante minutes. Pas plus!

Quand vous faites votre travail, le soir, offrez-vous une pause. Marchez, allez grignoter une tartine, tirez-vous la langue devant la glace. Vous serez beaucoup plus efficace après avoir soufflé.

En revanche, ne laissez pas votre mémoire trop longtemps en vacances. Si vous avez pris des notes pendant un cours, relisez-les autant que possible une demi-heure après, ou dans les trois heures qui suivent. Cette simple révision incruste les points importants dans votre tête.

Adapted from *Okapi*,
15–28 février 1993

QUESTION

Marks

Which two pieces of advice given in the passage do you find most useful?   (2)

Your pen-friend has sent you this birthday card.

QUESTIONS   *Marks*

(a) What does it advise you not to do?   (1)

(b) Why not?   (1)

© P & T Productions S.P.R.L., Bruxelles

A magazine asks three young people what they think of television.

Katia:	Moi, j'aime quand on est tous en famille pour la regarder. Ça m'apprend plein de choses.
Philippe:	Moi j'aime la regarder avec mes copains quand on ne sait pas quoi faire.
Pauline:	Moi, je l'aime parce que — en attendant mes parents quand je rentre du collège — je ne me sens pas toute seule.

© *Astrapi*, 1 novembre 1980

QUESTIONS   *Marks*

(a) Choose which picture best describes how each person likes to watch television, from picture A, B or C.   Katia ☐   Philippe ☐   Pauline ☐   (3)

(b) Why does each person enjoy television?
     Katia
     Philippe
     Pauline   (3)

On holiday in Canada with your family you decide to visit the Royal Ontario Museum (R.O.M.).
You pick up this leaflet.

R.O.M.
LE MUSÉE ROYAL DE L'ONTARIO

Des poteries et des pierres,
des oiseaux et des os. . .
vous pouvez toucher
à votre guise en explorant la

GALERIES DES
DÉCOUVERTES

Essayez la casque à visière d'une armure. Touchez à un os de dinosaure ou à des matières aussi
différentes que le bois et la porcelaine dans la Galerie des Découvertes, un endroit spécial
rempli de trésors à découvrir et à examiner.

Il est interdit d'apporter des manteaux, des parapluies et des grands sacs dans la Galerie des
Découvertes. Veuillez les laisser au vestiaire au rez-de-chaussée.
Il y a des textes en braille pour les handicapés de la vue.
La Galerie est accessible aux fauteuils roulants.

Heures d'ouverture
En semaine, réservée aux groupes scolaires.
La fin de la semaine et les jours fériés de 13 h à 17 h.

© Le Musée Royal de l'Ontario

QUESTIONS   *Marks*

(a) Why do you think it is called the 'Galerie des Découvertes'?   (1)

(b) What must you do with your coats?   (1)

(c) What facilities are available for those with disabilities?   (2)

(d) You want to visit on a Tuesday afternoon. Will this be possible? Give a reason for
     your answer.   (1)

Here is a poem about Félix Parfait. Read it, then answer the questions below.

Ton nom est Félix Parfait et tu es parfait

Ta mère est fière de toi
Mon fils Félix est parfait
Il ne mangerait
les spaghettis avec ses doigts

Ta maîtresse est fière de toi
Il ne rêve jamais pendant la journée
Il a toujours un crayon bien taillé
Il se tient toujours droit

Félix s'endort
sans jamais avoir peur du noir
dit son père
Je n'ai jamais besoin d'élever la voix

Oui mais. . .
un vrai Félix Parfait
Ça n'existe pas!!!

From *Félix Parfait et quelques autres enfants* by Bernard Waber, © l'école des loisirs 1971

QUESTIONS

Marks

(a) Give one reason why each of these people is proud of Félix.
His mother
His teacher
His father
(3)

(b) Why have you no reason to be jealous of Félix?
(1)

The remainder of this chapter consists of two tests. Each one is very similar to the exam. Do each test at a time when you can work undisturbed for 45 minutes and you feel quite fresh (not after you have done your other homework, but perhaps a Saturday or Sunday). Take note of how long you take to do each one.

Tackle each test the way you will in the exam, using the reading techniques you have practised in this chapter and allocating your time wisely.

TEST 1

Write your answers in ENGLISH. You may use a French dictionary.

Use your time wisely.	*Read the question carefully.*
Think ahead.	*Select the information you need.*
Use your dictionary with care.	*Check your answers.*

1. You are on holiday in France with your pen-friend, whose young sister shows you a poem she has written at school.

La liste des dix meilleurs jours de l'année

Il y en a seulement dix?

Le premier, naturellement,
c'est mon anniversaire.
Puis viennent Noël, Pâques,
le premier jour
des grandes vacances,
le jour de l'An,
le jour de ma fête,
l'anniversaire de Maman,
celui de Papa,
le premier jour du printemps
et celui de l'été . . .

— dans l'ordre où je te les dis.

Seulement dix!

From *Félix Parfait et quelques autres enfants* by Bernard Waber, © l'école des loisirs 1971

QUESTION

Which three of the days she mentions would you choose?

Marks

(3)

2. You pick up a leaflet advertising a new service.

EXCLUSIF

**Offrez un livre pour un anniversaire:
une fête . . .
un événement . . .**

La Poste se charge de son expédition, à la date de votre choix.

Renseignements et dépôt des livres de votre bureau de poste le plus proche.

© La Poste

QUESTIONS

Marks

(a) What new service is being advertised? (1)

(b) Where can you get further information? (1)

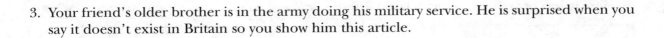

3. Your friend's older brother is in the army doing his military service. He is surprised when you say it doesn't exist in Britain so you show him this article.

SERVICE MILITAIRE: JUSQU'À 25 MOIS

Vous êtes une fille? Vous appartenez à un pays d'Europe de la Communauté Européenne? Alors, vous ne serez pas obligée de faire votre service militaire.

Si vous êtes un garçon, tout dépendra de votre nationalité!

Au Royaume-Uni, en Irlande et au Luxembourg, l'armée ne vous appellera pas obligatoirement sous les drapeaux, car dans ces trois pays, les soldats sont tous des professionnels.

Ailleurs, votre service militaire durera entre 10 mois (en Belgique) et 25 mois (dans la marine grecque).

© *Okapi*

QUESTIONS   *Marks*

(a) Which group of people do not do military service in any European country?   (1)

(b) Apart from Britain, in which two countries are people not obliged to do military
     service?   (2)

(c) What happens in the other two countries mentioned in the article?   (2)

4. You notice this article in a teenage magazine.

Vous êtes fatigués!

D'après des études menées par l'Inserm, la moitié des ados se sentent fatigués, 25% souffrent de maux de tête, un sur cinq avoue de se réveiller souvent la nuit, 10% font régulièrement des cauchemars. Au banc des accusés, les études scolaires arrivent en tête. Les médecins nous ont alertés il y a longtemps, mais la réforme n'est pas pour demain.

Alors patientez et consolez-vous en pensant à vos prochaines vacances . . . bien méritées!!!

Adapted from *Salut*, oct/nov 1992

QUESTIONS   *Marks*

(a) What is this article about, A, B, C or D?
    A Teenagers at school   B Teenage health
    C Teenage leisure   D Teenage holidays   (1)

(b) The article quotes four sets of statistics to support its findings. Copy and
     complete the table below.

50% of teenagers	
% of teenagers	suffer from headaches
20% of teenagers	
% of teenagers	regularly have nightmares

 (4)

(c) What does the article claim is the main culprit?   (1)

(d) What two pieces of advice does it give teenagers?   (2)

5. Here is part of an interview with Jason Priestley and Luke Perry about their attitude to school.

JASON: J'aimais beaucoup l'école où j'étais souvent le premier de la classe. Mais j'étais un élève en pleine rébellion: tête rasée, blouson de cuir, bottes et chaînes. Cela ne plaisait pas toujours aux professeurs.

LUKE: Je m'y ennuyais beaucoup. J'étais excellent en histoire, en sciences et en français. En revanche, je détestais les mathématiques.

© *OK PODIUM*, 19 avril – 2 mai 1993

QUESTION *Marks*

Which one expresses best your attitude to school? Why? (1)

6. You notice this competition in a magazine.

Réalisez votre rêve avec Salut et enregistrez un disque . . .

Cet été vous allez pouvoir réaliser votre rêve et devenir chanteur ou chanteuse.

Pour cela, il vous suffit de choisir une chanson connue, et d'enregistrer votre voix sur une cassette. Glissez dans une enveloppe cette fameuse cassette, une photo de vous et le bulletin réponse — et peut-être serez-vous le grand gagnant de ce super concours.

Si c'est le cas, Salut! vous invitera à venir à Paris, dans les studios des disques afin d'enregistrer un tube comme un chanteur ou chanteuse professionnel. Ensuite vous repartirez avec 100 cassettes de l'enregistrement de votre chanson, et des photos de votre extraordinaire aventure.

SALUT! CONCOURS
Réalisez votre rêve . . .
BULLETIN-RÉPONSE

Nom: ....
Prénom: ....
Adresse: ....
© *Salut* No 148

QUESTIONS *Marks*

(a) How could you enter the competition? (1)

(b) What should you include with your entry? (3)

(c) What prize can you win? Give details. (5)

TEST 2

Write your answers in ENGLISH. You may use a French dictionary.

Use your time wisely.	*Read the question carefully.*
Think ahead.	*Select the information you need.*
Use your dictionary with care.	*Check your answers.*

1. You are spending a holiday with your family in France. You wish to plan an excursion, so you look at the weather forecast in the newspaper.

MERCREDI Sur la moitié sud, assez beau temps. Les éclaircies seront plus belles et plus durables. Sur la moitié nord, encore beaucoup de nuages et de pluie.

A

B

C

☼	SOLEIL	⇨	VENT FAIBLE
	AVERSES	⮕	VENT FORT
	PLUIE		
	ÉCLAIRCIES		
≡	BROUILLARD		
	NUAGEUX		
	ORAGE		
✳	NEIGÉ		

© France-Soir

QUESTION

Marks

Which map, A, B, or C, describes the weather on Wednesday?   (1)

2. When planning a visit to a wildlife park you have the following brochures to study. Read the brochures and decide which park would best suit different members of the family.

Parcs animaliers

A. CHAMPREPUS

Parc zoologique — 20 km de Granville. Parc moderne où le confort et l'environnement des animaux sont les principales priorités. Sur un parcours de 2 km, vous découvrirez environ 90 espèces d'animaux. Parc d'attractions gratuit — Bar — Snack le midi en juillet et août. Ouvert du 15/03 au 11/11 tous les jours de 10 h à 18 h 30.
Tarifs: Adultes 38 F — Groupes scolaires 16 F.
Renseignements: Tél. 33 61 30 74

B. VILLIERS-FOSSARD

La Vallée aux Oiseaux — à 8 km de Saint-lô, la direction Cherbourg. Parc zoologique prédominance ornithologique. Plus de 160 espèces d'oiseaux. Parking, terrain de pique-nique, café, bar, crêpes et gaufres, jeux. Ouvert toute l'année.
L'été, tous les jours de 10 h à 19 h. L'hiver, le mercredi, samedi et dimanche de 14 h à la tombée de la nuit.
Tarifs: Adultes 35 F — Enfants 20 F — Groupes adultes 20 F — Groupes scolaires 8 F.
Renseignements: Tél. 33 57 75 22.

C. SAINT-SYMPHORIEN-DES-MONTS

L'EDEN-PARC. Sur la RN 176 à 7 km de Saint-Hilaire-du Harcouët (près du Mont Saint Michel). Parc animalier et collections de rhododendrons, azalées et hortensias dans un parc de château.
Exposition écologique de plein air en 20 tableaux. Aire de jeux et de pique-nique, bar, crêperie, magasin de souvenirs.
Ouverture du 15/05 au 11/11, tous les jours à partir de 9 h.
Tarifs: Adultes 28 F — Enfants 15 F — Groupes adultes 22 F — Groupes scolaires 12 F.
Renseignements: Tél 33 49 02 41

Adapted from *Ouest France*, juillet 1993

QUESTION

Marks

Choose which park, A, B or C, would suit each of these family members, and say why.

Grandfather likes flowers	(2)
Mother wants the cheapest entry fee	(2)
Brother prefers an amusement park	(2)
Sister is interested in birds	(2)

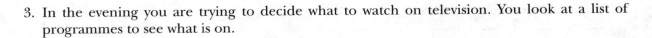

3. In the evening you are trying to decide what to watch on television. You look at a list of programmes to see what is on.

A.

ALLÔ, MARIE-LAURE

Émission de Marie-Laure Augry et Bernard Laine.

Marie-Laure Augry répond à vos questions, s'efforce de résoudre vos problèmes et de vous aider à réaliser vos projets.

Avec la participation des spécialistes de la rédaction: Jean-Pierre Berthet (justice), Jean-Michel Carpentier (social) et Alain Ammar (éducation).

Pour contacter «Allô, Marie-Laure» téléphonez au (16.1) 42.75.19.90; par courrier; TF1, «Allô, Marie-Laure» 19, rue Cognacq-jay, 75007 Paris.

B.

SAMEDI PASSION

Emission de Christian Quidet préparée et presentée par Gérard Holltz.

AVENTURE PASSION
Deux alpinistes allemands effectuent des escalades difficiles le long des parois des Dolomites.

AUTOMOBILE
Le coup d'envoi de la saison de formule 1 avec le Grand Prix du Brésil.

SAINT-ÉTIENNE — P.S.G.
Match de la trente et unième journée de Championnat de France de football.

C.

LE MONDE MERVEILLEUX DES ARAIGNÉES

Documentaire de Malcolm Penny.
Toutes les araignées ne sont pas des tisseuses de toiles, les autres se contentent de sauter sur leur proie, ou de les attraper au «lasso». Un monde fascinant. . .

D.

LA LIGNE DE CHANCE

Feuilleton américain
Jeff a été choqué et risque de retomber dans la drogue. Noel appelle Brandy en Californie pour l'alerter sur l'état de son père. Mais Cherry Lane intercepte le message. . .

Adapted from *Télé 7 jours* 25–31 mars 1989

QUESTIONS

Marks

(a) Which programme would you most like to see? (A, B, C or D) Why? (1)

(b) Which programme would you least like to see? (A, B, C or D) Why? (1)

4. You decide to watch this film.

Dimanche 26 mars

La cinq **5** **18.00 200 DOLLARS PLUS LES FRAIS**

ADIEU LAURA LEE
Sarah Butler, la directrice d'une petite entreprise, est persuadée que
la mort de l'une de ses employées n'est pas accidentelle. Aussi
décide-t-elle d'avoir recours au service d'un détective pour éclaircir le
mystère qui entoure cette affaire. . .

© *Télé 7 jours* 25-31 mars 1989

QUESTIONS

Marks

(a) Who is Sarah Butler? (2)

(b) Why does she employ a private detective? Give details. (3)

5. In a magazine you read this short feature article about the French comedy actor Gérard Jugnot.

François Gorget: *Avez-vous toujours eu
le sens de l'humour?*

Gérard Jugnot: Quand j'étais jeune, je
n'avais pas la force des muscles. Alors,
mon arme secrète, mon karaté à moi,
c'était l'humour. Cela pouvait claquer
comme une gifle!

© *Okapi*, 15–28 février 1993

QUESTION

Marks

How did his sense of humour help him when he was younger? (2)

6. In a magazine you find this cartoon. Your sister asks you to explain what it is about.

QUESTIONS   *Marks*

(a) In the first picture, why is Roméo pleased?   (1)

(b) Why is he less pleased at the end?   (1)

7. You read this letter from Marie.

Je m'appelle Marie, j'ai 14 ans et j'habite à Megève. Il y a quelque chose que je ne comprends pas et qui m'énerve. Lorsque je regarde la télévision ou que je lis n'importe quel journal, j'ai l'impression que la France entière habite en ville et tout particulièrement à Paris.

J'ai l'impression que les médias pensent que ceux qui habitent en montagne, comme moi, ou à la campagne, comme les paysans, ne sont pas cultivés...

Je pourrais aussi me moquer des citadins lorsqu'ils font du ski. Mais je ne le fais pas, par respect, et on dirait que, malgré leur grande culture, ils sont intolérants par rapport à nous.

Alors que, lorsque quelqu'un est cultivé, il doit avoir l'esprit ouvert...

© Okapi 509

QUESTIONS   *Marks*

(a) What kind of area does Marie live in?   (1)

(b) Why is she critical of the French media?   (5)

(c) What is her impression of city dwellers?   (2)

(d) How does she think someone who is really sophisticated **should** be?   (1)

CHAPTER THREE

Credit Reading

◼◻ GENERAL NOTES

If you have decided that it is really at Credit Level that you need more practice in reading, it would still be helpful to you to read what is said in Chapter Two about skimming, scanning and close reading, as you will need these skills in Credit Reading as well.

The first obvious difference between General and Credit Reading is that the passages are longer, some of them quite a bit longer. Do not be put off by the length — you will find that the heading and the questions will give you a general idea of what the passage is about and that the English questions will point you to the relevant part of the text.

Clearly, there will be more unknown vocabulary in these longer texts, but do not waste your time by looking up all the words you don't know in the dictionary. The questions will not require you to understand every word in the passage, so make sure you concentrate your efforts on what you need to know.

You can expect the sentences in the Credit Level passages to be more complex than those at General. To understand what is being said, you will need to make sure you give careful consideration to grammatical aspects such as the tenses of the verbs or the meaning of prepositions (to, from, above, below and so on).

You are given quite a lot of help with the first few passages, some of it is given in this chapter and some in Chapter Seven, then there are some passages for which no help is given. By the time you reach these, you should have a fair idea of how you should tackle a passage. Finally, there are two test papers, as in Chapter Two, for you to practise timing as well as applying your reading skills.

When you attempt one of the passages in this chapter, you should not be content just to answer all the questions correctly, or to find out what the correct answers are. Each passage should leave you better equipped to tackle the next one. You may develop a technique to deal with how to break up unknown words into their various parts, so arriving at the meaning of the whole word, or noting a particular French structure which puzzled you once, but which you hope to recognise next time you meet it. You may have met a number of new words. Clearly an increase in your vocabulary will save you time and help you, not just with reading, but with listening, speaking, and writing. So you should try to select something new from every text you work at. Be sensible in the choice you make — there's not much point in learning words which you are unlikely to meet again. Try to select words or structures which may well reappear in another passage.

One way to build up your knowledge of structures and vocabulary is to write each one on a card. Write the French word or words on the top left-hand corner of the card and its translation on the bottom right-hand corner. Find any suitable size of box and place the cards upright in it. Place a dividing card in the box. When you revise your vocabulary, start working at the front card. If you can remember it correctly place it behind the dividing card, but if you have difficulty put it at the back of the vocabulary cards, so that you will come across it again as you work through the cards. When you have got them all right, replace the cards behind the divider with the others, so that you can start afresh next time.

The first two passages in this Credit Reading section have been chosen to help you bridge the gap in length between passages in General and in Credit Reading. If you have decided to start your work with this book at the Credit section, have a look at the first passage and see if you have made a correct decision. If the passage seems difficult to you, go back and do the General passages first. If, on the other hand, it seems quite simple, you are advised to do it all the same, as a number of techniques are shown here which you will able to apply to longer and more complex texts.

CINÉMA
Batman 2
Le film

LE CÉLÈBRE HÉROS MASQUÉ EST DE RETOUR SUR LES ÉCRANS LE 15 JUILLET. ACTIONS ET EFFETS SPÉCIAUX GARANTIS!

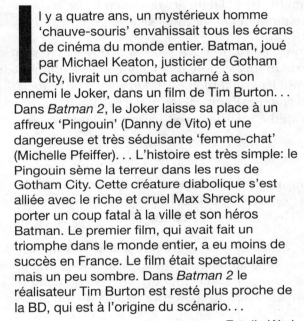

Il y a quatre ans, un mystérieux homme 'chauve-souris' envahissait tous les écrans de cinéma du monde entier. Batman, joué par Michael Keaton, justicier de Gotham City, livrait un combat acharné à son ennemi le Joker, dans un film de Tim Burton. . . Dans *Batman 2*, le Joker laisse sa place à un affreux 'Pingouin' (Danny de Vito) et une dangereuse et très séduisante 'femme-chat' (Michelle Pfeiffer). . . L'histoire est très simple: le Pingouin sème la terreur dans les rues de Gotham City. Cette créature diabolique s'est alliée avec le riche et cruel Max Shreck pour porter un coup fatal à la ville et son héros Batman. Le premier film, qui avait fait un triomphe dans le monde entier, a eu moins de succès en France. Le film était spectaculaire mais un peu sombre. Dans *Batman 2* le réalisateur Tim Burton est resté plus proche de la BD, qui est à l'origine du scénario. . .

Estelle Warin

La bande dessinée

Batman est né en 1939 dans un magazine de BD américain. Ses parents sont Bill Finger, scénariste, et Bob Kane, dessinateur. Pour créer Batman, Bob Kane s'est inspiré de Zorro, d'un homme ailé dessiné par Léonard de Vinci et d'un vieux film muet, *La chauve-souris*.

© *Je bouquine*, Bayard Presse Jeune, août 1992

Stage 1

In an exam paper, the heading in English may well be something like 'You read this film review in a magazine.' A quick glance at the French heading will reveal to you that it is an article about the film *Batman 2*.

Stage 2

What information do you expect to find in a film review? The names of the characters? The names of the actors who play them? The name of the director? Something about the plot? Something about the type of film? Critical/appreciative comment?

Read through the passage and see if you can find out information about the above, but don't worry if you can't find everything at this stage. Do **not**, at this stage, use the dictionary.

> **TIP** You have probably heard of *Batman 2*, you may indeed have seen the film, but be careful to base your answers only on what is written in the review.

Stage 3

You are now ready to look at the passage more closely. Read down to '. . . le Joker, dans un film de Tim Burton'. There are two main verbs in this section. Underline or note them. Do not bother at the moment about their meanings. Can you say what **tense** they are?

Now read from 'Dans *Batman 2*' down to 'les rues de Gotham City'. Note or underline the three verbs in this section. Again, at this stage, their meaning is not important. Their tense is. What is it? If you have included the Joker when you named the characters in *Batman 2*, you have got it wrong. Do you see why? Well spotted if you got it right! Now turn to Chapter Eight and check your answers to all the questions you have attempted so far.

Stage 4

You may not know some of the vocabulary in this review. Do **not** immediately reach for the dictionary. Look at each word to see if you can recognise any of it, and look at each phrase it is part of. Here are some examples.

un mystérieux homme 'chauve-souris'   You see first of all that 'chauve-souris' is an adjective describing a mysterious man. You notice that it is in inverted commas, which shows that there is something unusual about it. You know the word souris = mouse and that this is an article about **Bat**man. You can therefore deduce that chauve-souris = bat.

envahissait tous les écrans du cinéma   You probably know the meaning of 'les écrans du cinéma', so what do you think 'envahissait' could mean? Common sense will tell you that it must be something like 'appeared on' all the cinema screens, but you decide to check on its meaning in the dictionary. The ending -issait tells you that it is an -ir verb, so you look up envahir and you find it means 'to invade, overrun'. Actually neither of these words is very appropriate in English! Your original commonsense idea is good enough for comprehension here.

Batman. . ., justicier de Gotham City   Note the ending of the word justicier, -ier, an ending which along with -er and -eur is used very often when the noun refers to a person's trade or profession (e.g. fermier, épicier, boulanger, professeur). This then is a profession to do with 'justice'. As you check in the dictionary, you know the kind of meaning to expect.

livrait un combat acharné à son ennemi   You probably are not sure of 'livrait 'or 'acharné', but you will recognise 'combat' and 'ennemi'. The phrase has something to do with combat or a fight with an enemy. As with 'envahissait' you know it must be something like ' was carrying on a fight'. Your dictionary will tell you that livrer has a number of meanings. Do not take the first one 'to deliver'. Your commonsense is enough again.

Acharné is an adjective describing the fight. What kind of battle would you expect Batman to wage?

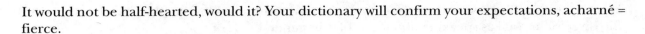

It would not be half-hearted, would it? Your dictionary will confirm your expectations, acharné = fierce.

Now try to work out:
le Pingouin **sème** *la terreur dans les rues* and *Tim Burton est resté plus proche de* **la bande dessinée.**

All this may seem to be time-consuming but, with practice, you may decide you do not require to look up the word at all, or, if you do look it up, these are the kind of things you can be thinking as you flick through the pages of the dictionary. If you have thought about it beforehand, you are less likely to make a wrong choice from the list of possibilities in the dictionary.

Stage 5   You might be asked:

QUESTIONS

Marks

(a) When did the first Batman film appear?   (1)
  • Look for a phrase which indicates a particular time in the past to give you your answer.

(b) Who are the villains in *Batman 2?*   (3)
  • Use the indication of marks to make sure you include all the information.

(c) What is the aim of the Penguin in the film?   (1)
  • You are not asked about what he is **doing**, but about his intentions. The clue here is the preposition 'pour' = 'in order to'.

(d) We now come to the part of the review where some kind of comment about the film is made. The question in this section could take various forms. *You could be asked straightforward questions like:*

   1. How successful was the first Batman film?   (2 points to be made here)
   2. What criticism was made of the first film?   (1 point)
   3. What different approach did the director adopt in the second film?   (1 point)

   You might be asked a question which combines the first two such as: What comments does the reviewer make about the success of the first Batman film?   (3 points)

   You might also be asked a question regarding your opinion, for example: Do you think the reviewer expects this film to be more successful than the first Batman film?   (1)

> **TIP**   You know, of course that there are no marks for saying 'Yes' or 'No'! The mark is given for explaining the reason.

You will notice that there are no questions about the information at the top and bottom of the right-hand column. Sometimes sections like these will be examined, but in quite a number of texts there are parts about which no questions are asked. Do not waste your time looking up words in such sections, once you are sure the information they contain is not essential.

Here is another film review. This time the reviewer concentrates on the plot, the characters and the director, as well as speaking about the film in general.

cinéma

Sortie le 1er avril

«HOOK» de Steven Spielberg

Steven Spielberg a imaginé la suite du livre de J.M. Barrie: *Peter Pan*. Dans *Hook*, Peter Pan est devenu adulte! Il s'appelle Peter Banning. Il est avocat, marié, il a deux enfants. Et surtout il a oublié son enfance. Mais son ennemi, le terrible capitaine Crochet ('hook' en anglais), se souvient de lui: comment oublier le seul garçon qui ait jamais osé le défier? Pour se venger de cette vieille humiliation, Crochet enlève les deux enfants de Peter Banning. Pour les sauver, Peter doit retourner au Pays de Nulle Part où l'attendent les pirates et leur chef le capitaine Crochet! Steven Spielberg est le réalisateur de *E.T.* et *Indiana Jones*. Il est l'un des maîtres américains du cinéma d'action et de science-fiction. Son nouveau film *Hook* rend hommage à l'univers féerique de J.M. Barrie qui est à la source de son inspiration. *Hook* a coûté soixante millions de dollars. Le résultat: un film spectaculaire, ses effets spéciaux impressionnants.

On y retrouve toute la magie d'un vieux conte dans le monde d'aujourd'hui. Aux États Unis c'est un véritable succès.

Estelle Warin

Le roman
Dans le livre de J.M. Barrie, Peter Pan est un garçon-lutin qui vit au Pays de Nulle Part. Un jour, il y emmène trois jeunes Anglais du XIXe siècle. Et les enfants découvrent un très étrange pays peuplé de pirates, d'indiens et de fées malignes. Ils font surtout la rencontre du capitaine Crochet, l'ennemi mortel de Peter Pan...
***Peter Pan* de J.M. Barrie (coll. Folio Junior). Les éditions Lattès ont réalisé un livre sur le tournage de *Hook*.**

© *Je bouquine*, Bayard Presse Jeune, avril 1992

Read through the passage quickly and note (a) the chief characters, (b) the minor characters and (c) the name of the director.

Grammar Hints

There are one or two phrases in this passage which might puzzle you because you have not met these particular structures before.

For example, you read 'le seul garçon qui **ait** jamais osé le défier'. If you meet something unfamiliar like this in the exam, do not worry about it. You will be able to arrive at the meaning of the phrase without necessarily understanding precisely each word in it. In this case, you can understand 'le seul garçon', you probably know 'osé', but, if not, check it quickly in the dictionary, and you can guess 'défier' from its resemblance to the English word. Put all these pieces of information together and you arrive at 'the only boy who ever dared to defy him'. This is all you need to know for comprehension purposes.

(The word 'ait' is in fact part of the present subjunctive tense of 'avoir'. It is used instead of 'a', and it has to be used here because of the emphasis put on 'seul'. You do not need to know all about this to understand the text!)

Now look at the phrase '. . . au Pays de Nulle Part où l'attendent les pirates et leur chef. . .' What might put you off here is that the verb has been put before the subject, and this is not the normal order in English. Do not be tempted to rely on your knowledge of the meaning of 'attendent', do **not** be tempted to read 'l'. . .' as 'he' and suggest that it is *Peter* who waits for the pirates and their captain. Two things tell you this cannot be right:

1. 'attendent' ends in **-ent** and must therefore have a plural subject, in this case the pirates and their captain.
2. ' l'. . .' is not he, but **him**, the object of the verb.

A correct rendering is then '. . . where the pirates and their captain are waiting for him.' Putting the verb before the subject in a clause beginning with 'où' is quite a common feature of French style — look out for it!

Now read the passage closely and answer the questions below. The questions are similar to those set in the exam, but some hints are included to help you at this stage.

Use the dictionary as thoughtfully as possible. Some help is given with the following words and phrases in Chapter Seven. You may not need help, as you may know the words already. You may prefer to work them out for yourself, but when you have finished the questions, have a look at Chapter Seven and see if you can learn anything from what is written there.

la suite	**avocat**	**enlève les deux enfants**	**impressionnante**

TIP Remember to:
— see if you can recognise part of the word;
— establish what part of speech (noun, verb, adjective and so on. . .) you are looking for;
— think of the meaning of the whole phrase, not just isolated words.

QUESTIONS

Marks

(a) What has happened between the book *Peter Pan* and the film *Hook*? (1)
 • Note the tense of the question to help you with the answer.

(b) Describe the Peter who appears in the film. (5)
 • Note the number of marks given.

(c) Why does Captain Hook remember him? (1)
 • Find the French phrase for 'remember'. The information required follows this.

(d) What does he do for revenge? (1)
 • Find the French word that looks like the word 'revenge'.

(e) Why must Peter go back to Never-Never-Land? (1)
 • Remember the preposition 'pour'?

(f) What does he find when he gets there? (1)

(g) In what kind of films does Steven Spielberg excel? (2)
 • Note — two marks.

— and finally a question which asks you to explain something

(h) Why do you think the film *Hook* has had such success in the U.S.A.? (2)
 • You will find the word 'succès' is the last word in the passage, so you will have to look in the text immediately before it. Have you noticed there are **two** marks for this question?

Here is an example of the kind of article that you might read in a magazine and which can give you advice about something. Cast your eye quickly over the article and questions and say, in one sentence, what this article is about.

L'argent de poche

En ce début d'année, il est recommandé de régler les petits problèmes quotidiens et en particulier la question de l'argent de poche. Vous avez sûrement dépensé tous vos sous, eh oui, les cadeaux, ça coûte cher! Vous voilà fauchée. Mais allez donc faire comprendre cela à vos parents! Et pourtant il vous faut une augmentation, votre argent de poche est insuffisant. Pas la peine de criser! Expliquez-leur calmement que vos besoins ont augmenté mais ne leur demandez tout de même pas la lune!

COMMENT PERSUADER VOS PARENTS?

Avant d'aborder la question de l'argent de poche, vérifiez que c'est le bon moment. Attendez qu'ils soient détendus. Entamez la discussion sur des sujets variés pour amener la conversation sur l'argent. Le tout, c'est d'être très diplomate. Ne commencez pas par citer les sommes «énormes» qu'ont vos copines. Vous allez les indisposer. . . Vous préparez une liste de tout ce que vous achetez par mois et vous leur prouvez MATHEMATIQUEMENT que ce qu'ils vous donnent chaque semaine (ou chaque mois) est insuffisant. Le cinéma, l'essence pour le Vespa, les classeurs Naf Naf, les disques, les babioles, les bonbons, tout ça mis bout à bout, ça coûte une fortune! Il n'y a pas d'argument infaillible mais insistez sur le fait que gérer votre argent de poche et bien planifier vos dépenses sont des moyens excellents pour vous responsabiliser. Apprendre à tenir un budget d'une façon autonome vous oblige à réfléchir à intégrer la valeur de l'argent. Comment résister à une telle démonstration? Mais ne soyez pas trop matérialiste tout de même! Ne commencez pas à négocier vos bisous, votre tendresse, vos bonnes notes. Tenez compte également de leurs moyens financiers. Ajustez votre demande à ce qu'ils peuvent vous donner. Ne proposez pas un chiffre la première, attendez leur offre. Si cela n'est pas assez, marchandez un peu. L'important, c'est de s'entendre sur un forfait: tant par mois et vous êtes libre de le dépenser comme vous voulez!

© *OK*, 11–17 janvier 1993

The article divides into two parts — the break is shown by the heading to the second part. This heading tells you what the second part is about. What, again in one sentence, is the purpose of the first part?

Can you say if this article has male or female readers in mind? (Don't waste time on this if you don't see it very quickly. You will find the answer in Chapter Eight.)

One very common way of giving advice is to use the imperative (command) form of the verb, which, as you know, ends in -ez. Cast your eye over the article and see how many of these commands you can spot. (You should find about a dozen.)

You now should have a very fair idea of the general content of the article.

The phrase 'attendez qu'ils soient détendus' is explained in Chapter Seven as are the following vocabulary items, which you will not normally find in a small dictionary or where the meaning given will perhaps not help you.

criser	responsabiliser	autonome	bisous	tendresse

Now answer the following questions:

QUESTIONS

Marks

(a) Why is this an appropriate time of year to raise the question of pocket money with your parents? (1)

(b) What should you do before you even open negotiations? (3)
- Find the word in the passage for **before**. Note the number of marks.

(c) Name four things on which teenagers might want to spend money. (4)
- Obviously, in an exam you find four things which you know. Here you can extend your vocabulary by working out the others.

(d) The writer suggests some things you should not do in the course of negotiations. (2)
State two of these.
- Again, for practice, find more if you can.

(e) Which argument do you think might impress parents? (1)
- Find as many as you can, but remember just to write **one** in the exam.

(f) What does the writer consider the most important part of the negotiations? (1)

The next article (on page 36) is an example of the longer type of text which may come up in the examination. It is what the French call a *'fait divers'*, a local news feature, a story about some kind of accident, traffic scheme, new shop opening, a story about a well-known person, a local improvement or whatever.

In any article which tells a story, the verbs are particularly important as they take us through the story stage by stage. You will find that in French newspapers and magazines the tense which carries the story is usually the present tense, whereas in our own language it would normally be the past. The French use this 'historic present' tense to make the account more vivid and dramatic, as though the incident were taking place under your very eyes.

In an examination, although the story is told in the present tense, the questions may very well be put in the past tense, which is more natural speech.

There is a note in Chapter Seven about the structures 'Prévenus, les parents. . .' and 'Epuisé, les lèvres violettes, Nicolas. . .' which you may find useful to consult.

In dealing with a longer passage, it is a good idea to break it up into sections. Sometimes the questions which are set will help you to do this. Here we will consider the article one paragraph at a time, but first see if you can find out very generally what the story is all about.

Tout à coup, la terre s'écroule sous les pieds du petit Nicolas

Grâce au pompier Jean-Luc Lagueyt, Joëlle a pu retrouver indemne son petit garçon de 4 ans . . .

Ce mercredi-là, un soleil superbe éclaire le petit village de Pouyallet, dans le Médoc. Nicolas Ferreira, un mignon bambin de 4 ans aux joues rebondies, est heureux: il peut aller jouer avec les enfants des voisins, les Maroszek. Il y a Bertrand, qui a le même âge que lui, Anne-Sophie, 8 ans, comme sa sœur Mélanie, et Pauline, 13 ans, comme son autre sœur, Aurélie. . . Une correspondance d'âge qui a rapproché les deux familles.

Après avoir joué un moment dans le jardin, les enfants s'aperçoivent tout à coup que Nicolas a disparu! Ils l'appellent, mais seuls des pleurs lointains leur répondent. Aussitôt Mme Maroszek court chez d'autres voisins, les Lafforgue, qui découvrent ce qui s'est passé: alors que Nicolas jouait près d'un vieux puits condamné, la terre s'était écroulée sous ses pieds!

Avant l'arrivée des pompiers, les Lafforgue envoient une corde au garçonnet, mais il est trop petit pour se la nouer autour du corps. Au-dessus de lui, Nicolas entend toutes ces voix qui lui disent de ne pas bouger. Lui, d'habitude si désobéissant, écoute cette fois tout ce qu'on lui dit.

Prévenus, les parents de Nicolas sont là. Joëlle, la maman, est au bord de la crise de nerfs et Séraphin, le papa, à plat ventre près du trou profond de 4 m, lui parle durant une heure et demie, pour le rassurer.

L'état du terrain étant inconnu, le risque d'éboulement est réel. Pour récupérer l'enfant, il faut donc passer par le puits et creuser un tunnel jusqu'à lui. Un pompier, Jean-Luc Lagueyt, descend alors dans le puits. Il aperçoit la lumière de la lampe électrique qu'on a descendue à Nicolas et, au burin, il creuse un passage. Tout cela lui prend une heure. . .

Epuisé, les lèvres violettes, Nicolas est finalement hissé à la surface et transporté à l'hôpital. 'C'est un miracle,' raconte Séraphin avec émotion, 'nous avions tellement peur de le perdre. . .'

Quant à Jean-Luc, le courageux pompier, pour lui, ce sauvetage restera toujours différent des autres. En effet, lui-même père d'un petit garçon du même âge, l'image de son propre enfant se confondait sans cesse à celle de Nicolas.

BRIGITTE DUCASSE

Stage 1

Read the title and the line below it. From the first, we learn what happened. What did happen? From the second, we learn the identity of the three people who are involved. Who are they?

Stage 2

Now read the first paragraph. It gives a number of background facts. From the midst of all of these, find out what is important in the story. Is it the weather? Is it the physical appearance of Nicolas? The ages of his sisters and friends? No, it is what he is going to **do** that day. What is he going to do?

Stage 3

Read the second paragraph. Look for the verbs and say:
(a) what the children do (three things);
(b) what Mme Maroszeck does;
(c) what the Lafforgues do.

Note that there is a change of tense towards the end of the paragraph. This is because the writer is telling us what **had** happened. What had happened?

> **TIP** Be careful to be accurate here. Do not jump to the conclusion, because you know or find out
> that puits = well, that Nicolas had fallen **down** the well.

Stage 4

Read paragraph 3. It tells us of the Lafforgues' efforts to rescue Nicolas.
(a) What do they do, and why does it not succeed?
(b) What are the people telling Nicolas to do?
(c) In paragraph 4, Nicolas' parents come on to the scene.
(d) What does his father do?

Stage 5

Paragraph 5 brings us to the actual rescue.
(a) What is considered the only safe way to rescue Nicolas?
(b) What does Jean-Luc do?

Paragraph 6 tells us what happens to Nicolas, and what his father says about it all. What happens? What does he say?

Stage 6

The last paragraph tells us of Jean-Luc's reaction to the whole affair. Why will he never forget this rescue?

Stage 7

Why do you think the journalist gave us all the information about weather and families in the first paragraph?

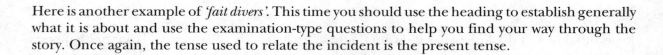

Here is another example of *'fait divers'*. This time you should use the heading to establish generally what it is about and use the examination-type questions to help you find your way through the story. Once again, the tense used to relate the incident is the present tense.

Il plonge dans le canal:
4 personnes sauvées

De notre correspondant Andrew Wareing

Il est des sauveteurs modestes, des hommes pour qui risquer sa vie pour sauver celle d'autrui semble la chose la plus naturelle. A Roubaix, Christian Rigaut, 42 ans, fait partie de ces anonymes qui, une fois leur geste accompli, n'aspirent qu'à retrouver leur petite vie tranquille. Lui a sauvé quatre personnes de la noyade, dont un bébé de un an et demi, en plongeant dans un canal quatre fois consécutives. Puis il est rentré à son bureau pour se changer et se remettre au travail.

Christian Rigaut est penché sur un dossier dans une salle de son entreprise d'import-export, quand il entend un bruit violent. Grand, les cheveux blonds coupés court, très mince, il relève la tête: le choc d'une voiture tombant dans l'eau. A quelques dizaines de mètres, sous ses fenêtres coulent les eaux noires du canal de Roubaix, l'un des cours les plus pollués de France.

La conductrice d'une automobile, Catherine Scrite, 26 ans, infirmière, vient d'avoir un malaise au volant. Dans la voiture qui s'enfonce rapidement c'est la panique. Il y a ses parents, Michel et Germaine Hus, 69 et 64 ans, et Pierre, son bébé de 18 mois. Le véhicule n'est pas encore complètement englouti que Christian Rigaut plonge. Il a traversé la rue en courant. Il ne prend même pas la peine de se déshabiller, tout juste le temps d'enlever ses chaussures. L'eau est trouble, mais cela ne l'empêche pas d'arriver à ouvrir une portière et à se saisir du petit Pierre. Il dépose l'enfant sur le bord, puis trois fois, se rejette dans le canal.

'Heureusement, l'eau n'était pas trop froide... J'ai pu remonter le bébé et ses grands-parents sans mal. Pour la conductrice, c'était plus difficile, car elle était inanimée et avait bouclé sa ceinture de sécurité. J'ai cru manquer de souffle, mais j'ai réussi à la dégrafer, puis à la sortir de sa voiture.' Modeste, il tient à rajouter: 'Mais, vous savez, je ne sais pas très bien nager.'

The journalist is reflecting in the first paragraph on the incident and uses one or two structures and expressions which may not be familiar to you. Help is given in Chapter Seven with the following items:

Il est des sauveteurs   **celle d'autrui**   **anonymes**   **une fois leur geste accompli**   **lui**

QUESTIONS   *Marks*

(a) What, according to the writer, does the modest rescuer want to do after he has carried out his heroic action?   (1)

(b) How did Christian Rigaut show that he comes into this category?   (2)

(c) What explained the noise he heard as he sat at work?   (1)

(d) Why is the water in the canal at Roubaix black?   (1)

(e) What caused the accident?   (1)

(f) What do you know about the four people in the car?   (3)

(g) State two things which show that Christian did not waste any time.   (2)

(h) Why did Christian find it more difficult to rescue the driver?   (2)

(i) What surprising fact does Christian tell us at the end?   (1)

Another kind of article which comes up fairly frequently in the examination is an interview, either with someone well known or with an 'expert' on some aspect of modern life. In the article below, the magazine *Okapi* is interviewing Michel Platini about how he became a professional footballer. In this type of article, the questions put by the interviewer, as well as the English examination-type questions, will help you to find the information required. As you can see from the interviewer's questions, there are three sections — Michel Platini's beginnings in football, the attitude of his family and his decision to become a professional.

Interview with
Michel Platini

Okapi: *Quand avez-vous commencé à jouer au football?*

Michel Platini: Du plus loin que je me souvienne, j'ai toujours voulu faire du football: j'ai commencé à taper dans un ballon vers 5 ou 6 ans.

J'adorais jouer dans la rue avec mes copains. Le matin, je continuais encore à jouer sur le chemin de l'école. Parfois, le soir, j'allais même me coucher avec mon ballon. Vous voyez, c'était une vraie passion!

D'ailleurs, chez moi, tout le monde aimait le sport: à Jœuf, la petite ville de Lorraine où j'ai grandi, mes grands-parents italiens tenaient un café qui s'appelait *Le café des sportifs*. Ma mère, elle avait fait du basket. Mon père, lui, entraînait l'équipe de football.

© Okapi

Okapi: *Votre famille vous a sans doute beaucoup encouragé. . .*

Michel Platini: Moi, mes parents ne me disputaient jamais quand je revenais d'une partie de football avec mon pantalon déchiré.

Je me souviens qu'une fois, j'ai cassé les carreaux de la voisine avec mon ballon. Ce jour-là, mon père ne m'a pas interdit de continuer à jouer. Sinon, j'aurais peut-être tout arrêté: je ne serais jamais devenu footballeur.

Okapi: *Comment avez-vous décidé de devenir footballeur professionnel?*

Michel Platini: À 10 ans, j'ai disputé mon premier match amateur. Pour moi, c'était un grand moment. La nuit d'avant, je n'ai pas réussi à fermer l'œil. Pourtant, tout s'est bien passé: j'ai marqué les deux premiers buts. Aujourd'hui encore, c'est le plus beau souvenir de ma carrière!

Depuis ce jour-là, j'ai rêvé de jouer devant beaucoup de monde, et au plus haut niveau! J'ai tout fait pour me perfectionner, pour devenir plus adroit. Quand j'ai eu 16 ans, j'ai choisi de me lancer à fond dans le football: mon père m'a autorisé à arrêter mes études, pour entrer au club de l'Association Sportive (A.S.) Nancy-Lorraine. C'était une décision difficile à prendre. Rendez-vous compte: la carrière d'un footballeur professionnel dure en moyenne . . . cinq ans. Cinq ans seulement!

Heureusement, on m'a fait confiance. Tout s'est bien passé. J'ai réussi à jouer pendant quinze ans à Nancy, à Saint-Étienne, à la Juventus de Turin, et bien sûr, en équipe de France.

QUESTIONS

		Marks
(a)	How did Michel's passion for football show itself when he was young?	(3)
(b)	What sporting links did his family have?	(3)
(c)	What two facts show his family's support for his football?	(2)
(d)	Why is his first amateur match the outstanding memory of his career?	(1)
(e)	Why was his decision to become a professional footballer a hard one?	(1)
(f)	What justified the decision in his case?	(1)

Another kind of text which may appear in an examination is a poem or the words of a song. The questions asked will, as with any other kind of text, require you to find factual information from the text, and will probably ask you to say something also about the mood of the poem or song, the message it conveys or about how you respond to it. Notice that in some cases the letter 'e' may be replaced by an apostrophe so that there are the right number of syllables to fit the music.

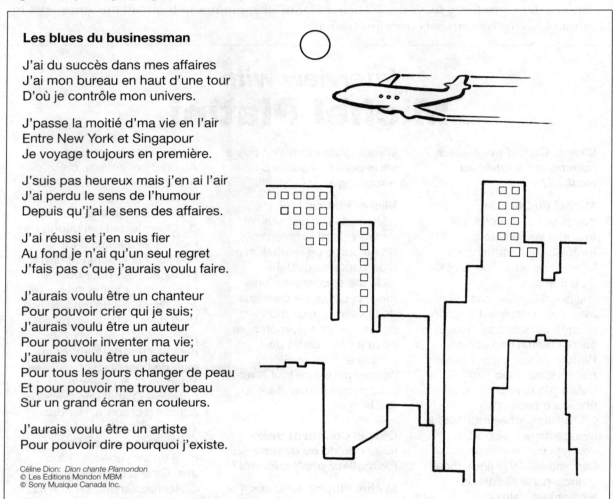

Les blues du businessman

J'ai du succès dans mes affaires
J'ai mon bureau en haut d'une tour
D'où je contrôle mon univers.

J'passe la moitié d'ma vie en l'air
Entre New York et Singapour
Je voyage toujours en première.

J'suis pas heureux mais j'en ai l'air
J'ai perdu le sens de l'humour
Depuis qu'j'ai le sens des affaires.

J'ai réussi et j'en suis fier
Au fond je n'ai qu'un seul regret
J'fais pas c'que j'aurais voulu faire.

J'aurais voulu être un chanteur
Pour pouvoir crier qui je suis;
J'aurais voulu être un auteur
Pour pouvoir inventer ma vie;
J'aurais voulu être un acteur
Pour tous les jours changer de peau
Et pour pouvoir me trouver beau
Sur un grand écran en couleurs.

J'aurais voulu être un artiste
Pour pouvoir dire pourquoi j'existe.

Céline Dion: *Dion chante Plamondon*
© Les Editions Mondon MBM
© Sony Musique Canada Inc.

QUESTIONS

Marks

(a) Where is the businessman's office and what impression does this give him? (2)

(b) What arrangement about his travels lets us know that he is rich? (1)

(c) What price has he paid for his business success? (1)

(d) What does he regret? (1)

(e) Choose one of the types of person mentioned and give a reason why he would have liked to be like that. (2)

(f) What, for you, is the message of this song? (1)

If you have worked through all these passages, you should be well equipped to tackle the following passages without any further explanatory notes.

You read this article about the popularity of skateboarding.

LA FOLLE HISTOIRE DU SKATE...

La planche à roulettes est un pur produit des années soixante. Le bébé appelé skateboard est né en 1962. Deux surfeurs professionnels, Mickey Munoz et Phil Edwards constatent qu'en absence de «bonnes vagues», ils ne peuvent pas s'entraîner. Ils confectionnent alors des modèles réduits de leurs planches et les équipent de roues de patins à roulettes. Nom de baptême: roll-surf. Le petit nouveau de «la glisse» fait fureur sur toute la côte ouest des Etats-Unis. Puis sur tout le continent américain.

1965–1970: LE FLOP

En France, la nouvelle planche a peu de succès: les roues de caoutchouc ne sont pas adaptées au macadam et la mode s'évapore aussi vite qu'elle est arrivée.

1977–1980: LE BOOM!

Il faut attendre 1977 pour voir la planche revenir au galop. Raisons du «boom»: l'uréthane et le polyuréthane, qui révolutionnent la composition des roues. Les chiffres dépassent toutes les prévisions en 1978, 20 millions d'adeptes aux Etats-Unis, 500 000 pratiquants en France. Le 27 décembre 1977, la Fédération française de skateboard est reconnue officiellement. Dans les grandes villes de France, fleurissent les «*Skateparks*», des installations spécialement dessinées pour les fanatiques du skate: on y trouve des «*Half-pipes*» (demi-cylindres en béton), des «*Banks*» (berges inclinées à 40°) et des «*Pools*» (cuvettes)! Et puis soudainement, en 1979, le souffle retombe.

© *Phosphore*, février 1988

Les skateparks ferment leurs portes. Celui d'Issy-les-Moulineaux est transformé en . . . camping!

1987–19. . .: LE STREET STYLE

Le skateboard revient. . . Cet été, Eric Berton (champion de ski acrobatique) organise des stages à Val Thorens, mais la nouvelle vague du skate est essentiellement urbaine et violente. Le style «Street» envahit la ville. Mais pour combien de temps?

QUESTIONS

Marks

(a) How did the first skateboards come to be made? (5)

(b) Why did skateboarding not succeed in France initially? (1)

(c) What caused the boom in skateboarding in 1977? (1)

(d) What happened to one skatepark when the popularity of the sport fell again? (1)

(e) Where do you find the new wave of street-style skateboarding? (1)

(f) What suggests that the writer is doubtful that this new popularity will be lasting? (1)

In a magazine you read this interview with Alexandra Tuttle.

Alexandra Tuttle est Américaine et vit à Paris. Son métier? Journaliste. Elle travaille pour un prestigieux magazine américain, *Time*. Nous lui avons demandé de nous parler de Paris.

Okapi: *Comment avez-vous fait la connaissance de Paris?*

Alexandra Tuttle: Je connais Paris depuis l'âge de cinq ans. Avec mes parents, nous passions les mois de juillet ici et à Saint-Tropez. Mes parents sont des amoureux ardents de la France. Ils ne vont en vacances . . . qu'en France.

Aussi loin que remontent mes souvenirs, Paris est une ville que j'ai toujours connue et aimée. Après avoir fini mes études supérieures en Angleterre, je me suis installée tout naturellement à Paris, pour y vivre.

Okapi: *Alors, que pensez-vous de Paris?*

Alexandra Tuttle: C'est une très belle ville. Il est beaucoup plus facile de vivre à Paris qu'à New York. Ici, à Paris, les gens ont l'air de s'amuser, d'être en bonne santé.

Le rhythme de vie est moins dur qu'à New York, plus humain. Les immeubles sont à six ou sept étages. Et il y a, dans les rues, une animation extraordinaire, malgré le climat médiocre.

Okapi: *A votre avis, qu'est-ce qui caractérise cette ville?*

Alexandra Tuttle: Pour moi, c'est son atmosphère «méditerranéenne». Il y a toujours une foule de gens dans les cafés, qui restent là des heures, et discutent de tout et de rien. Les terrasses des cafés, ça n'existe pas aux Etats-Unis.

Okapi: *A quelle époque de l'année préférez-vous Paris?*

Alexandra Tuttle: C'est comme si vous me demandiez si je préfère mon père ou ma mère! Paris, au printemps, pour ses lumières subtiles, Paris à Noël pour ses décorations de fête.

Les premières années où je venais à Paris, au moment de Noël, j'étais triste parce qu'il n'y avait aucune mise en scène dans les rues, alors que, chez nous à New York, c'est merveilleux et très chaleureux.

Et puis, peu à peu, les Parisiens ont commencé à décorer leur ville, avec des lumières, des petits rubans argent et or. Maintenant, sur un certain nombre d'avenues, les arbres sont recouverts de lumières. C'est féerique, même plus beau qu'à New York.

© Okapi

QUESTIONS

Marks

(a) What is Alexandra's profession? (1)

(b) Why is it that she got to know Paris at an early age? (2)

(c) When did she come to live in Paris? (1)

(d) State three differences that she mentions between Paris and New York. (3)

(e) What does she say about Paris cafés? (3)

(f) What used to disappoint her about Paris at Christmas time? (1)

This magazine article, which talks about relationships between young people and their parents, catches your attention. First of all, read the section entitled *'Les sujets de discorde'*.

LA GUERRE N'AURA PAS LIEU! *Vous et vos parents*

LES SUJETS DE DISCORDE

Les sorties: Tout dépend bien sûr de votre âge, mais, en général, vos parents sont très inquiets quand vous sortez. Ils vous voient exposés à toutes sortes de dangers et n'ont pas forcément tort: c'est en dehors de la maison que vous pouvez être tentés par la drogue, que vous pouvez vous planter en voiture après une soirée en boîte de nuit, avec une bande de copains plus ou moins éméchés par l'alcool, etc.

A chaque sortie, vous avez donc droit à une série de questions assommantes du style: *'Avec qui tu sors?'*, *'Qui est-ce qui conduit?'* *'A quelle heure tu rentres?'* Et si,

© *Salut* No 151, 25 août 1993

par malheur, vous dépassez l'heure promise, vos parents sont victimes des pires inquiétudes.

L'argent: Évidemment vous n'en gagnez pas. N'empêche qu'il vous en faut un minimum pour vos loisirs, et c'est à vos parents qu'il revient de vous en donner. Voilà un objet de dispute permanent: *'Moi, à ton âge, je n'avais pas le dixième par mois de ce que tu me demandes pour une soirée. . .'* Certes, mais entre-temps, l'inflation est passée par-là. Il est vrai aussi que la société a beaucoup changé: le mode de vie a énormément évolué et avec cela les besoins.

QUESTIONS

Marks

(a) What particular dangers are mentioned that your parents fear for you when you go out? (2)

(b) What do your parents do that annoys you when you are going out? (1)

(c) When are your parents especially worried? (1)

(d) What reply can you make to your parents' statement that they didn't have anything like the money you expect to have? (3)

Now look at the section on page 44 entitled *'Comment mettre vos parents dans votre poche?'*

LA GUERRE N'AURA PAS LIEU!

Vous savez que vous allez être en retard?
Informez-en vos parents par téléphone.
Vous leur épargnerez bien des angoisses.

COMMENT METTRE VOS PARENTS DANS VOTRE POCHE?

Pour réduire les tensions de façon significative, voici quelques règles:

La vérité: Croyez-moi, ça paie toujours! Dans la mesure du possible, il faut leur dire la vérité, à savoir où vous êtes allées, ce que vous avez fait, qui vous avez rencontré . . . je vous conseille même de devancer leurs questions. Il convient de rassurer vos parents pour gagner leur confiance.

L'argent, ça se négocie! Donnez-leur l'impression que l'argent qu'ils vous donnent n'est pas un dû et que vous n'êtes pas totalement dépendants. Aider aux tâches

© *Salut* No 151, 25 août 1993

ménagères, garder votre petit frère, laver la voiture de votre père pourraient devenir des activités payées ou qui vous vaudront leur reconnaissance. . . Cela vous permettrait de neutraliser les éventuelles menaces concernant vos résultats scolaires, vos sorties. . .

Horaires à respecter: Essayez de rentrer à l'heure prévue lorsque vous sortez. Si vous avez dit que vous serez rentrées à 1 h, n'oubliez pas que l'on vous attendra avec angoisse dès 1 h 15. En cas de retard certain, n'hésitez pas à passer un coup de fil! Sinon, c'est sûr, vous aurez du mal à éviter la crise en pointant le bout de votre nez chez vous.
Docteur M.

Pour que votre foyer ne devienne pas un terrain de batailles, il suffit de peu, de rassurer vos parents en leur montrant que vous êtes responsables.

QUESTIONS

Marks

(a) What is the first piece of advice you are given to reduce tension? (1)

(b) State two of the things the writer suggests you do to earn your pocket money. (2)

(c) What should you do if you know you're going to be late? (1)

This article on dieting catches your eye in a magazine.

JE VEUX MAIGRIR!

Voici venir les beaux jours... C'est le moment d'essayer les maillots de bain et rien ne vous va. Bref, vous avez trop de poids et selon les cas, vous devriez perdre entre 2 et 10 kg.

L'AVIS DU DOCTEUR M.

'Il faut manger à sa faim des aliments équilibrés'

Ce qu'il ne faut pas faire:
Observer une période de jeûne
Que cela dure un jour ou trois ou quatre, c'est stupide. Vous allez perdre du poids sur la balance mais vous allez le reprendre immédiatement après. Et en prime, vous aurez eu toute la souffrance du jeûne. Opération nulle dont vous sortirez perdant(e).

Les régimes pamplemousse, ananas et autres.
Bien sûr, en ne mangeant qu'une sorte d'aliment (même des pâtes et des pommes de terre), vous finirez par maigrir mais en mettant votre santé en danger. En agissant ainsi votre corps n'aura pas tout ce dont il a besoin pour sa croissance. De plus dès que vous cessez ce type de régime, vos kilos reviendront aussi vite qu'ils se sont envolés.

© Salut

Ce qu'il faut faire...
Evitez de maigrir trop rapidement: maigrir de 3 à 4 kilos doit se faire en plusieurs semaines voire plusieurs mois. Il est complètement stupide d'imaginer que l'on va perdre 3 kilos en une semaine! Si l'on y parvenait, cela serait dangereux et en même temps inefficace.

Mangez matin, midi et soir à votre faim des aliments équilibrés: voilà une manière intelligente de conserver les joies de la table et aussi ... d'être en accord avec sa silhouette.

QUESTIONS

Marks

(a) Why might readers be thinking of dieting at this moment? (2)

(b) What are the doctor's objections to fasting as a means of losing weight? (2)

(c) What price might you pay for losing weight on a special diet? (1)

(d) What does the doctor say about the rate at which you should lose weight? (2)

(e) How does he think you should eat? (2)

(f) What benefits will this bring? (2)

The remainder of this chapter consists of two tests. Each one is very similar to the exam. Do each test at a time when you can work undisturbed for **one hour** and you feel quite fresh (not after you have done your other homework, but perhaps on a Saturday or Sunday). Take note of how long you take to do each one.

Tackle each test the way you will in the exam, using the reading techniques you have practised in this chapter and allocating your time wisely.

TEST 1

Write your answers in ENGLISH. You may use a French dictionary.

Use your time wisely.	*Read the question carefully.*
Think ahead.	*Select the information you need.*
Use your dictionary with care.	*Check your answers.*

1. Read this article about a very unusual service that is being offered.

MA VIE EST UN ROMAN

Nos parents nous racontent leur vie par bribes... Petit à petit, leur histoire se dessine. Mais, au-delà de nos grands-parents, nous ne savons plus rien des nôtres qu'une vague légende.

Une femme a eu l'idée de servir de lien entre ceux qui ont envie de laisser des traces écrites de leur vie et d'autres qui sauront

© *Elle*, 11 avril 1983

les aider à le faire. Elle s'appelle Simone Wallich et a créé une maison d'édition pas comme les autres: *J'étais une fois*. 'Les gens aiment raconter leur vie. Et souvent le font bien, de vive voix. Mais quant à prendre la plume, c'est une autre histoire. . .' Et même, que faire du manuscrit? Depuis quelques mois, il existe une **solution**. *'J'étais une fois'* envoie chez l'auteur quelqu'un dont le métier est de savoir écouter. L'auteur a préparé son récit et l'enregistrement se fait en trois séances d'une heure et demie. Les bandes sont décryptées et réécrites par des professionnels. Puis l'œuvre est **publiée** à quelques exemplaires. Et de la première à la dernière page, pour chaque feuille écrite, une autre est laissée blanche, pour que ce livre de la vie reste ouvert. Aux commentaires, aux photos, à toutes sortes de documents. . .

L'opération, on s'en doute, prend du temps: **quatre à cinq mois**. Et elle n'est pas donnée: il faut compter près de quinze mille francs pour un, dix ou trente exemplaires du roman de sa vie. En somme, Simone Wallich a eu une riche idée, en ces temps où le téléphone a remplacé les lettres . . . qui, elles au moins, pouvaient se garder.
S. de M

QUESTIONS

Marks

(a) How much does the writer say we know about our forebears? (1)

(b) What link does Simone Wallich hope to provide? (2)

(c) What can people do quite well? (1)

(d) What solution does the company *J'étais une fois'* offer to those who find difficulty in writing their story? (4)

(e) Why are blank pages left in the resultant work? (2)

(f) What two drawbacks are there in this system? (2)

(g) Why is such a record particularly important nowadays? (2)

(h) How would you explain the title of this article? (1)

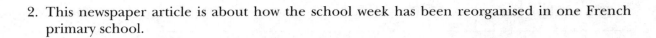

2. This newspaper article is about how the school week has been reorganised in one French primary school.

RENTRÉE PRÉMATURÉE POUR LES 200 ENFANTS DE LÉRÉ, DANS LE CHER

LA SEMAINE DE 4 JOURS

Le prix à payer: dix jours de vacances en moins

De notre envoyé spécial
Gilles CARVOYEUR
LÉRÉ

En ce deuxième jour de septembre, une atmosphère quelque peu inattendue règne dans la cour de l'école primaire de Léré. Avec une semaine d'avance, la petite école communale, située au cœur du village, au pied de l'église et tout près de la mairie, a repris du service. Le groupe scolaire compte six classes de cours élémentaires, première et deuxième année.

«Tout le monde est là», dit, satisfaite, la directrice, Josette Ravault, en poste à Léré, ce chef-lieu de canton situé au nord-est du Cher. Sauf un élève, ajoute-t-elle, qui rejoindra ses petits camarades dans deux jours au plus tard.

«En janvier dernier», continue-t-elle, «l'inspection académique du Cher a officiellement informé les enseignants du canton de la mise en place d'un rythme scolaire sur quatre jours, les lundis, mardis, jeudis et vendredis avec des horaires inchangés.

En contrepartie, on grignote sur les vacances, dix jours sont déduits, un aux vacances de Toussaint, deux à Noël, en février et à Pâques et les grandes vacances sont repoussées de trois jours au 11 juillet. Cette formule a recueilli l'adhésion de tous les parents. Et les enseignants.»

«La rentrée se passe en douceur», constate Josette Ravault, institutrice depuis trente ans, dont vingt années passées à Léré. Bien sagement, les quelque 200 élèves ont repris en rangs bien ordonnés — deux par deux — le chemin de la classe.

Cartable neuf au dos, trousse remplie de crayons et de stylos au look Disney, l'ambiance est déjà studieuse. «Signe des temps» remarque Josette Ravault, «on n'entend plus guère de pleurs. En juin, les enfants qui entrent en cours préparatoire découvrent leur nouvelle école et ainsi la déchirure avec les parents est moins douloureuse dès que la porte de la classe s'est refermée.»

A 11 h 30, fin de la matinée, synonyme pour beaucoup de premier déjeuner à la cantine du village, avant de reprendre l'école dès 13 h 30 pour trois autres heures de découverte du savoir.

© *France-Soir*, 3 septembre 1993

QUESTIONS

	Marks
(a) What is different this year about the first day back in the primary school in Léré?	(1)
(b) Why is the head teacher pleased?	(2)
(c) What decision had the education authorities taken?	(3)
(d) What arrangement has been introduced in return for this?	(4)
(e) What impression do you have of the pupils' behaviour?	(1)
(f) How does Josette Ravault explain the fact that there are hardly any tears on the first day?	(3)
(g) What is your opinion of the school day these primary pupils have?	(1)

3. This article makes some suggestions about helping those who are less fortunate than ourselves.

Solidarité

Pour un monde à visage humain...

Vous aimez le sport? Pourquoi ne pas prendre contact dans votre municipalité avec les associations pour handicapés et organiser des matchs de basket avec eux. Les personnes âgées ont aussi souvent besoin d'aide, vous pourriez sûrement leur proposer des services domestiques qu'ils récompenseront peut-être par un peu d'argent de poche. Et dans le cadre de vos études avez-vous déjà songé à soutenir par votre correspondance un prisonnier politique ou un enfant, en contactant Amnesty International. Ce serait aussi une occasion unique de perfectionner une langue vivante étudiée à l'école. Quant aux vêtements que vous ne portez plus, ou aux jouets dont vous vous êtes lassés, pourquoi ne pas les apporter à Emmaus avant Noël et faire ainsi le bonheur des plus démunis? Certes, vous êtes régulièrement sollicités par des quêtes diverses: cartes postales de l'Unicef, timbres de la Croix Rouge, Journée des aveugles etc. Mais il est aussi possible d'aider directement les sans-abri ou les gens qui n'ont rien à manger en offrant votre aide personnelle à des organisations comme les Restos du Cœur.

Tout cela peut paraître ridiculement idéaliste, mais voilà, le monde de demain ressemblera à ce que chacun est prêt à en faire dès aujourd'hui. En faisant tous des efforts, on peut améliorer le quotidien de ceux qui souffrent de la guerre (comme en Yougoslavie), des régimes politiques inhumaines, mais aussi de la maladie. Des choses toutes simples, par exemple, le verre récupéré dans les containers mis à notre disposition dans les villes et les communes permet de recueillir des fonds pour la lutte contre le cancer.

Sans un minimum de souci de l'autre, il n'y a pas de vie en société possible...

© *Salut*

QUESTIONS

Marks

(a) What does the writer suggest you do if you have sporting interests? (2)

(b) What benefit to yourself might helping old people bring? (1)

(c) How might you improve a foreign language studied at school? (2)

(d) How can you help poor people at Christmas? (2)

(e) Apart from contributing money to various charities, how else might you help? (1)

(f) State two areas where the writer feels we can improve the lot of other people. (2)

(g) What simple action helps to provide money to fight cancer? (1)

(h) Why do you think the writer has called this article *'Pour un monde à visage humain...'*? (1)

TEST 2

Write your answers in ENGLISH. You may use a French dictionary.

Use your time wisely.	*Read the question carefully.*
Think ahead.	*Select the information you need.*
Use your dictionary with care.	*Check your answers.*

1. This article gives you some advice about what to do in your summer holidays.

Votre argent des vacances

Les grandes vacances approchent, et avec elles les longues journées sans école, sans travail. Un régal! À condition de bien les remplir. La plupart du temps, il faut bien dire que les activités intéressantes sont loin d'être gratuites. Sans compter toutes les petites envies qu'on aimerait bien se passer. Bref! pour vivre des vacances heureuses, il faut de l'argent. Et il n'est pas toujours facile d'en dénicher. Si vous avez déjà trouvé un job pour l'été, tout est pour le mieux. «Cette année, je m'y suis pris à l'avance», explique Aurélien. «L'année dernière, j'ai passé les vacances complètement fauché, alors que mon meilleur copain a travaillé au mois de juillet. Résultat: au mois d'aôut, je n'ai pas pu le suivre dans ses sorties. Il m'invitait de temps en temps, mais c'est gênant de ne jamais pouvoir payer. Cette fois-ci, ce sera différent. J'ai posé ma candidature dans une banque il y a plusieurs mois déjà, et j'ai été pris. Je suis ravi!»

© OK

QUESTIONS

Marks

(a) What must you do to make the long summer days really enjoyable? (1)

(b) What is the snag about getting the most out of them? (1)

(c) Contrast the experience of Aurélien and his friend last year. (3)

(d) How did Aurélien feel about his friend's invitations? (1)

(e) How are things going to be different for him this year? (2)

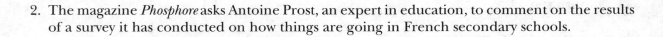

2. The magazine *Phosphore* asks Antoine Prost, an expert in education, to comment on the results of a survey it has conducted on how things are going in French secondary schools.

Phosphore: *D'après notre enquête, les lycées n'ont pas si mauvaise réputation: parents et élèves se disent plutôt satisfaits de la qualité de l'enseignement... Que pensez-vous de ce résultat?*

Antoine Prost: Il ne m'étonne pas. Les lycées font leur métier correctement. L'enseignement français a su éviter toute une série de changements que l'on trouve dans d'autres pays. En Suède par exemple, on a réduit les heures de suédois pour obliger les garçons à apprendre la couture. Aux États-Unis on a pratiquement abandonné l'enseignement des langues étrangères car elles n'étaient pas exigées à l'université. En gros, notre enseignement fonctionne bien.

Phosphore: *En revanche, les jeunes et leurs parents critiquent vivement les conditions matérielles de travail.*

Antoine Prost: En effet. Ils ont tout à fait raison de dénoncer la saleté ou la surcharge des locaux.

Quant aux emplois du temps, le système d'options mis en place en 1981 a abouti à des horaires monstrueux. On est obligé de mettre des cours après 16 heures ou à l'heure du déjeuner.

© *Phosphore*, février 1988

Phosphore: *Autre point noir: les rapports entre élèves, enseignants, administration, c'est moyen-moyen... L'ambiance, est-ce vraiment si important?*

Antoine Prost: Certainement. L'objectif au lycée est de bien travailler et un professeur ne peut apprendre aux élèves à travailler s'il n'a pas un bon rapport avec eux.

Phosphore: *Les critères d'après lesquels parents et élèves jugent les lycées vous semblent-ils judicieux? La discipline vient en premier pour les parents, suivie du taux de réussite aux examens. Les clubs sont pratiquement placés en dernier. Êtes-vous surpris de cet ordre?*

Antoine Prost: Non, elle me semble logique. Les adultes estiment important que les jeunes soient dans un milieu où l'on est poli, où l'on se tient bien, bref où la discipline est forte.

On ne peut pas leur reprocher non plus leur attitude envers la réussite aux examens, c'est une des fonctions du lycée. Quant aux clubs, il est évident qu'ils sont secondaires. Dans un horaire déjà occupé à 100%, quelle place peuvent-ils avoir?

MICHÈLE SALTIEL

QUESTIONS *Marks*

(a) Why is Antoine Prost not surprised that parents and pupils are generally satisfied with French schools? (1)

(b) Describe one of the two errors he thinks have been made in other countries. (2)

(c) What do parents and pupils criticise strongly? (1)

(d) What does Antoine say about:
   (i) the criticisms of the buildings, and
   (ii) when some classes in the timetable have to take place? (4)

(e) Why does he agree that the general atmosphere in a school is important? (1)

(f) What are the two most important factors by which parents judge a school? (2)

(g) What does Antoine say about the place of clubs in a school? (1)

(h) From all that he has said, what, in your opinion, is important for Antoine in a school? (1)

3. This magazine article is about the child star Anna Chlumsky. Read it and answer the questions that follow.

Anna Chlumsky

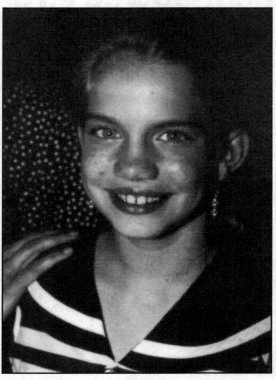

Anna est née il y a onze ans à Chicago d'un père chef cuisinier et d'une mère sans profession. Mais, trop tôt, le couple Chlumsky divorce avant de donner à Anna un frère ou une sœur. Monsieur part dans un restaurant parisien exercer ses talents et madame veille sur son petit ange blond et gérant, dès son dixième mois, sa carrière de 'mannequin-cadum'. De photos en spots publicitaires. Anna devient, en plus d'être une brillante élève, une si jolie petite fille que les Japonnais la remarquent et viennent jusqu'à Chicago la chercher pour tourner une pub. Elle n'a alors que 7 ans!

Pendant toutes ces années, l'agenda de Miss Chlumsky est, comme on dit dans le show-biz, 'over-booké'. Très studieuse à l'école, elle multiplie ses expériences aussi bien au théâtre qu'à la télévision et apprend le chant, la danse, le piano et la clarinette, jusqu'au jour où . . . après un casting de mille candidates, Howard Sieff choisit Anna pour incarner Vada Sultenfuss, la petite amie de Macaulay Culkin.

Toujours aidée et soutenue par sa maman, Anna prit sa première grande expérience ciné très au sérieux et son partenaire Dan Aykroyd ('SOS Fantômes') a même révélé qu'Anna connaissait pendant le tournage aussi bien son rôle que celui des autres comédiens! C'est ainsi qu'une star est née. Le film triomphe aux USA et remporte un gros succès en France.

Même si les portes du septième art s'ouvrent toutes grandes devant Anna, il n'est pas question pour elle d'abandonner l'école: *'Si je peux le faire, bien sûr que j'aimerais continuer le cinéma, mais je pense avant tout à mes études. J'adore l'école et c'est pour moi très important!'* Elle est d'ailleurs très cultivée et son étonnante maturité lui permet aussi bien de parler d'arithmétique que de peinture ou de cinéma. Elle apprend (en plus!) l'allemand et connaît par son père, assez bien le français.

© *Salut* No 124, 12 août 1992

QUESTIONS

Marks

(a) What do we learn about Anna's parents? (5)

(b) What did her good looks lead to when she was just seven years old? (2)

(c) Apart from her appearances in the theatre and on television, what other talents does Anna develop? (1)

(d) What shows that Anna took her first big role in a film very seriously? (1)

(e) What is her attitude to school work? (1)

(f) What do we read about her that shows us that her interests are not confined to show business? (3)

4. You read the words of this song in a magazine.

Peut-être qu'en septembre

Les jours passent sur la maison d'en face
Je pense à toi
Je pense à toi

Ça ne fait pas un an tout à fait
Que tu as fermé
Les volets

Moi, j'ai décidé de t'attendre
Peut-être qu'en septembre
Tu reviendras
Moi, j'ai décidé de t'attendre
Peut-être qu'en septembre
Tu seras là

Ta guitare tu sais
Est toujours là
Et elle s'ennuie autant que
moi

Les jours passent septembre
est déjà là
Je pense à toi
Je pense à toi

Moi, j'ai décidé de t'attendre
Peut-être qu'en septembre
Tu reviendras
Moi, j'ai décidé de t'attendre
Peut-être qu'en décembre
Tu seras là.

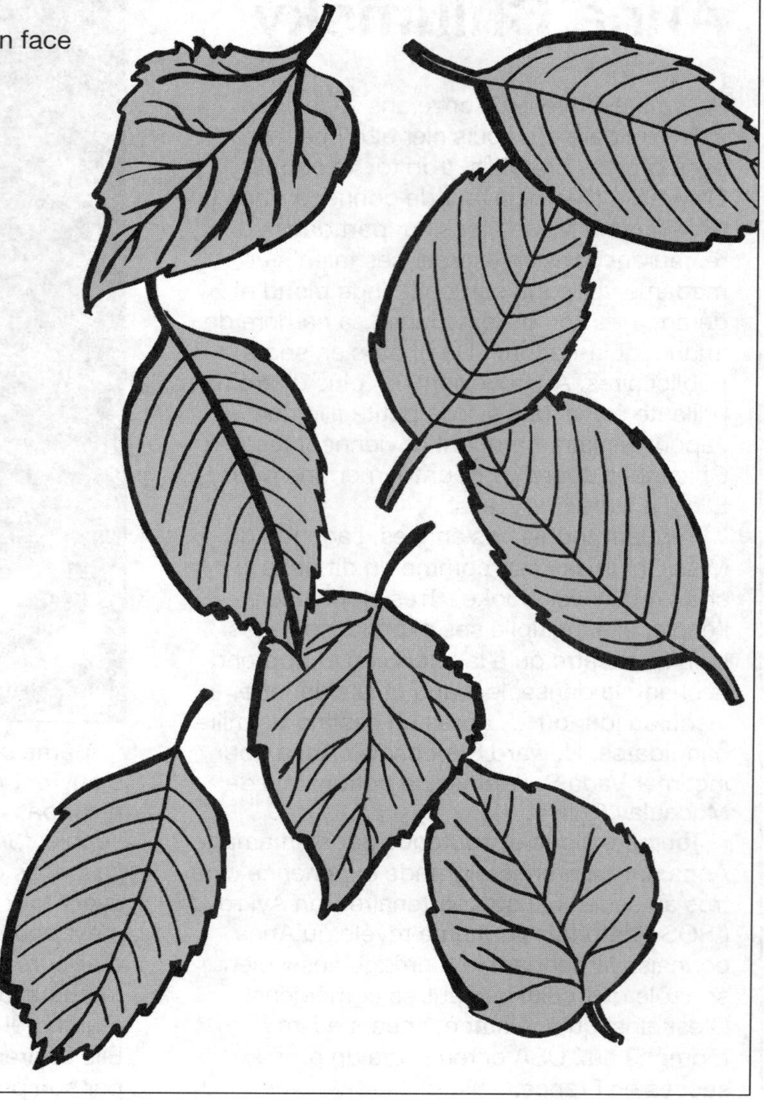

Singer: Hélène Rolles
Author: Jean-François Porry
Composers: Jean-François Porry/Gérard Salesses
© 1992 Abedition

QUESTIONS

Marks

(a) What situation does the singer describe in the first two verses? (4)

(b) What is she hoping? (1)

(c) Why do you think she mentions a guitar? (1)

(d) What happens when September comes? (1)

(e) Do you think the singer has given up all hope at the end? (1)

CHAPTER FOUR

General and Credit Speaking

▮▯ GENERAL REMARKS

Unlike assessment in Reading, Listening and Writing, where there are separate tests at different levels, the Speaking Tests are common to all candidates. The way in which Speaking is assessed is also quite different from the way the other three aspects of the French Standard Grade are tested. For Reading, Listening and Writing you have set tests on a particular day, but for Speaking your teacher is looking to give you a grade which gives a picture of your everyday performance — a continuous assessment. This 'ongoing assessment' will be made throughout your year as you take part in normal classroom activities.

Here are some of the class activities for which, from time to time, your teacher will give you a grade:
- conversation
- group discussion
- interview
- speaking with or without preparation
- simulation
- role play
- production of short theatre pieces (drama sketch)
- game playing
- short rehearsed or unrehearsed reporting.

There will also be many opportunities to practise speaking in class *without* the task being assessed when your teacher will hear you as often as possible and advise you as to how to improve your performance. In these and in the activities which are assessed, your teacher will be considering such points as:
- how well you can help to keep a conversation going;
- how often the person speaking to you has to repeat or rephrase what is being said;
- how much help you have to ask for;
- how well you can initiate in conversation;
- how easily you make yourself understood;
- how fluent you are;
- how good your pronunciation and intonation are;
- how accurate your use of language is;
- how varied your vocabulary and structures are.

Whatever the activity, you will be expected to use language which is not only varied and accurate but also appropriate to the situation. You do this already when you make a difference between the way you speak to your classmates and the way you speak to the teacher.

You should try to monitor your own performance and make every task an improvement on the one before. Here are two things you can do throughout your course to improve your speaking skills.

1. To improve your performance, especially with regard to accuracy and variation of vocabulary and structures, you should prepare and learn vocabulary lists under topic headings, useful structures and joining phrases, as described in Chapter Six, Credit Writing — see page 81. Try to get into the habit of bringing them into your speaking activities, so that you become able to use them quite naturally. This needs more practice than in writing because you do not have so much time to think about what you are going to say.

2. After a speaking activity in school, you may have some ideas that you wish you had expressed, so go over the activity at home and see how you could have said more, or said some things better. This will help to prepare you better for the next time.

If you want a good Speaking grade, you must be prepared to take a very active part in all the speaking exercises you have in class, even if you are by nature rather a quiet person. It is important for your overall award that you do well in Speaking, because it is double-weighted — you count your Speaking grade twice and add it to your grades for Reading and Listening, then divide by four to arrive at your overall award. (Remember that Writing is optional, and not taken into account for the overall award.)

A number of the skills required for Speaking are also useful for Writing and you should do the exercises described in this chapter at the same time as you practise to improve your writing skills.

We'll look now at some of the exercises which you might wish to improve and see how you can do so in class and at home.

INDIVIDUAL ACTIVITIES

One thing you can easily practise at home is giving a talk or report. In this type of activity, you will be stating facts and expressing your opinions, just as you do in Credit Writing. When you write something, either one of the exercises in this book, or something you are asked to do in school, you should try giving a talk on the same topic shortly afterwards. Let a short time elapse between the written and the spoken exercise so that you are not just reciting something by heart. On no account 'read' a talk — it will sound most unnatural and your pronunciation will suffer. You can make the talk from notes if you need something to jog your memory, but these notes should not be complete sentences. For example, you might want to say in your talk 'Je n'aime pas passer mes vacances avec mes parents', so you could write as a note 'vacances avec mes parents', and you should then be able to express how you feel about that.

If you can, record your talks. Listen to them and, if you think you can do better, record them again. Do not use the pause button while you think what to say next. Just let the pauses stay there and, if they are very long, think of how you could shorten them ('Eh bien', 'Voyons', 'Alors' etc.). Remember that short pauses are quite acceptable. If you have a French pen-pal, you might try exchanging tapes instead of letters.

In general, your talks should be related to the other work you are doing, but here are some additional topics on which you might try giving a talk or report.

Mes passe-temps
La ville/le village où j'habite
Ce que je fais pour aider à la maison
Mon argent de poche
Mes rapports avec mes frères/sœurs
Une ville/un pays où je voudrais vivre
Une excursion en groupe scolaire

In some exercises you will want to tell a story about something. For that you will need to have a good knowledge of verbs.

Here is a very simple story for you to practise on.

Ma journée

TASKS 👆

Stage 1

Tell this story in the present tense, just using verbs with no trimmings. Here is a list of the verbs you will need:

se réveiller	**se laver**	**s'habiller**	**quitter**	**se lever**	**prendre**
rentrer	**arriver**	**parler**	**se coucher**	**faire**	**écouter**

Stage 2

Tell the story again, this time linking the various verbs by using phrases like:

puis   ensuite   après cela   mais   et

and mentioning the various times.

Stage 3

Repeat the story, this time saying what you think and feel about some of the activities. (J'aime. . . C'est intéressant. . . A mon avis, c'est . . . — or any appropriate phrases from your list.)

Stage 4

You are now going to tell the same story, but this time in the perfect tense. Look at the list of verbs given in Stage 1 and note which ones take 'être'. (Remember that reflexive verbs take 'être'.) Go through the story with just the verbs — 'Hier matin, je me suis réveillé(e) . . .' — then join up and expand your sentences as before.

For further practice, tell the story of an ideal Sunday you have recently spent.

Here is a similar exercise about holidays.

Vacances au bord de la mer

TASKS ☞

1. Imagine that this is what you did on holiday this year. Tell the story in the perfect tense 'L'année dernière j'ai passé mes vacances au bord de la mer. . .' Make sure of the verbs first, then expand in whatever ways you can.
2. Do the same thing, but make the subject 'nous' instead of 'je'.
3. Now imagine that this is what you are going to do this year. Tell the story in the future tense, using **aller** + infinitive. 'Cette année je vais passer. . .'.

For further practice, give an account of holidays where everything went wrong — weather, transport, company, accommodation.

PAIRED ACTIVITIES

It is obviously much more difficult to practise for these on your own! If you have a friend or a member of your family you can work with, this will be very helpful, but even on your own, there are some things you can do to improve your performance. You will have to be prepared to provide both parts of the conversation, and to help you remember your rôle you could sit on one chair when you are playing one person and change to another for the other person.

You could do this kind of thing either after you have had a conversation in school or to prepare yourself for one which you will be doing the next day.

Transactions

One advantage of learning a foreign language is that you can obtain goods and services more easily when you are abroad. You will also find it useful if you are employed in this country in a job where you deal with the public. It is possible to make yourself understood in a variety of situations using a small number of phrases.

As you see, it is possible to manage on a few fixed phrases and this is what your teacher will be looking for at Foundation level. This is, after all, the foundation on which you base your language learning.

There is, however, no set list of phrases and vocabulary which you have to learn for Standard Grade. This enables you to build up your own resources. You will remember them much more easily if you learn how to use them as you go along. Aim to leave your French class having mastered at least *three* new phrases every day — from reading passages, listening texts or examples your teacher gives you. Practise these new phrases as often as possible so that using them feels natural.

You will want to choose the most suitable phrase for the situation you are acting out and, the wider your range of vocabulary, the greater choice you'll have. Which of these would you decide to use if you were asked to book a room for your family in a French hotel?

You will also be expected to react appropriately to the answers you are given.

What would you say?

(i)   (ii)   (iii)

In the first instance (i), it is not clear that you have understood how expensive the rooms are. Perhaps you are just saying 'Thank you' because you cannot think of what else to say.

In the second picture **(ii)**, you have certainly understood the answer. But your response is rather abrupt and, depending on the tone of voice you used, may sound very rude.

In the third reply **(iii)**, you have shown clearly that you understood the price. Furthermore you have taken the initiative and shown that you can negotiate to obtain what you want.

TASKS 🎭 How many different ways do you know in French to ask:
- how much something costs;
- where something is;
- if something is available;
- for an item;
- when something happens?

Check that you know at least one different way of speaking in a formal and in an informal situation.

Rien n'est Simple!

Even the simplest transaction can be complicated if you cannot obtain exactly what you want. Suppose you have been told to find out whether there is a swimming pool near your hotel. You have prepared your question:

Il y a une piscine près de l'hôtel?

The answer, however, is not the simple set of directions you expected but:

Je regrette, mademoiselle, il n'y en a pas. Mais vous en trouverez une à Nantes — c'est à dire à 30 kilomètres d'ici. Il faut prendre le bus.

Ne panique pas! The secret here is not to carry on regardless with your prepared answer — possibly something like, 'Merci, madame,' but to relax and think out an appropriate reply.

You can murmur 'Euh ... oui ...' while you consider what to say. This shows the person you are speaking to that you are thinking and haven't just dried up.

It can also help to repeat part of what the person said. This is a useful check that you have heard correctly and also lets you work out what to say next.

Here this might be something like:

*Euh. . . Il faut prendre le bus?
Et . . . où peut-on prendre le
bus pour Nantes, madame?*

The more practice you have in adapting to the unexpected, the easier you will find it. When you are working in class, try to change your partner frequently. Otherwise you will expect the same old responses each time. If you go over a task several times never try to produce the 'perfect' answer. It doesn't exist! Instead, try to change the details each time, introducing as many obstacles as you can.

You are not expected in any case to be able to speak flawless French. We all make mistakes from time to time even in our own language. What is important is to communicate as well as possible and above all to keep talking.

TASKS How would you respond to the following 'complications'?

1. You want to find out the time of the next train to Paris. You are told:

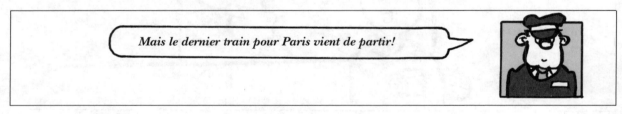

Mais le dernier train pour Paris vient de partir!

2. You have invited your French host to dinner in a restaurant. When you arrive you are told:

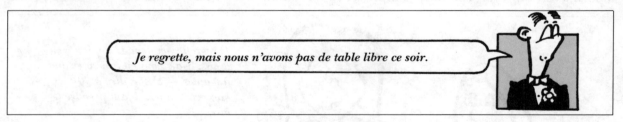

Je regrette, mais nous n'avons pas de table libre ce soir.

3. You ask a French student visiting your school to come with you to a burger restaurant. She replies:

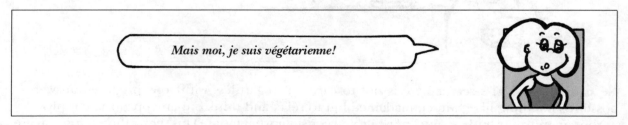

Mais moi, je suis végétarienne!

4. Your host has asked you to do some shopping. You are told at the grocery:

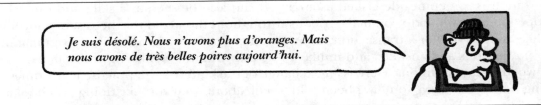

> *Je suis désolé. Nous n'avons plus d'oranges. Mais nous avons de très belles poires aujourd'hui.*

5. You have seen a T-shirt you would really like to buy, but the banks are closed and you can't cash your traveller's cheques. Could you persuade your exchange partner to lend you some money?

Remember to use language which is appropriate to the situation.

Rôle Play

From time to time you may be asked to act out a situation in which you play the part of someone else. Read the question carefully to get some idea of the situation and of your 'character'. Before you start, consider whether you are saying **'tu'** or **'vous'** to the person you are addressing.

TASKS ☺

Work with a partner or use the technique of the two chairs which was described earlier to practise both parts in these situations.

- Ton ami(e) vient de rentrer de ses vacances. Tu veux savoir comment ça s'est passé.
- Tu voudrais faire du baby-sitting. Le monsieur/la dame qui dirige le service te pose des questions.
- Tu as passé toute la soirée à jouer avec les jeux vidéo. Explique à ton prof d'histoire pourquoi tu n'as pas fait tes devoirs.
- Tu as passé un week-end épouvantable. Tu en parles à ton ami(e).
- Tu es allé(e) en ville et tu as manqué le dernier train/autobus. Tu téléphones à tes parents.

Conversation

Conversation is sometimes described as an art. It can also be seen as a skill, and one which if developed in class will help you make friends throughout the world for the rest of your life.

Unlike an interview or a transaction, a conversation does not consist only or even mainly of a series of questions and answers; and unlike a rôle play you will be playing yourself, exchanging your own ideas and opinions. Here is an exchange of the kind you will practise many times when learning new vocabulary. You have been told to talk about what you like doing at school and in your free time.

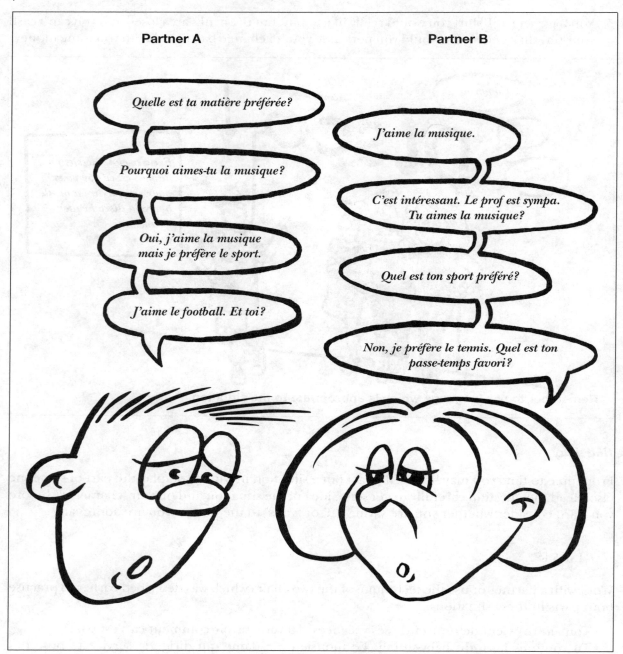

You will notice that this 'conversation' is not going anywhere. Each participant asks or answers a question but does not really develop the idea or show an interest in his or her partner's replies. Finally partner B abruptly changes the subject in order to fulfil the instructions they have been given.

Once you are confident about the new language you have learned, your conversation on the same topic may be something like this:

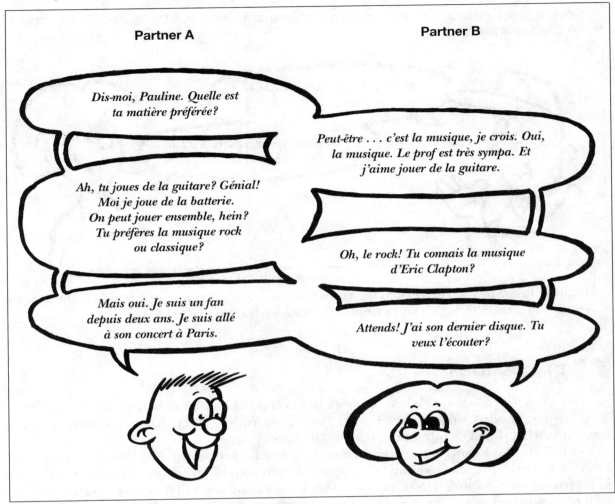

Partner A

Partner B

Dis-moi, Pauline. Quelle est ta matière préférée?

Peut-être . . . c'est la musique, je crois. Oui, la musique. Le prof est très sympa. Et j'aime jouer de la guitare.

Ah, tu joues de la guitare? Génial! Moi je joue de la batterie. On peut jouer ensemble, hein? Tu préfères la musique rock ou classique?

Oh, le rock! Tu connais la musique d'Eric Clapton?

Mais oui. Je suis un fan depuis deux ans. Je suis allé à son concert à Paris.

Attends! J'ai son dernier disque. Tu veux l'écouter?

Notice that this time the speakers moved on quickly from the subject of school to spend more time on the part that really interested them — their mutual interest in music. At this stage the instructions you are given are only a guideline to help yout think about areas you might want to talk about. You can move away from them if you want . . . as long as you keep talking in French.

The speakers still asked each other questions but also included expressions of opinion (Génial), suggestions (On peut . . .) and invitations (Tu veux . . .?). There were also more pauses, because a real conversation does not follow a script, and expressions like 'Dis-moi' to attract the other person's attention. Addressing your partner by name (monsieur or madame if it is your teacher) shows that you are interested and makes your dialogue sound more lively. You should also show that you are interested by looking at your partner as you speak. This means of course that you cannot be looking at your book or prepared notes. These are skills you can go over in class until you are confident about using them in an unscripted task.

Remember that you are not expected to produce perfect grammatical French in a speaking task . . . as long as you keep talking.

TASKS 🎭

1. How do you think the conversation above would have evolved if the participants had gone on to discuss an interest in tennis rather than music?

2. Imagine at least two different ways in which the following conversation could develop.

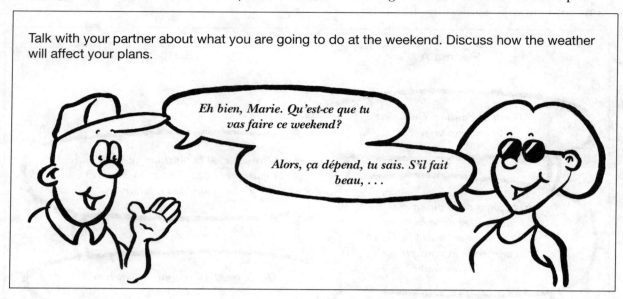

Talk with your partner about what you are going to do at the weekend. Discuss how the weather will affect your plans.

Eh bien, Marie. Qu'est-ce que tu vas faire ce weekend?

Alors, ça dépend, tu sais. S'il fait beau, . . .

3. Look at Task 2 again. How would the conversation change if you were talking to your teacher instead of a friend? Again, try to think of at least *two* variations.

DISCUSSIONS

Are you a talker or a listener? When you work in a group it is important to do both. The skills you have learned in other subjects, like English, will apply in the French class too — listening with interest to what is said by others and responding appropriately.

You will also find many similarities between classroom discussions and Credit Writing tasks. Both ask you to consider a topic and to express your opinions and you may well find one skill useful in preparing for the other. However, when you are speaking you will have less time to think out your responses and naturally you will not be expected to be as grammatically accurate . . . as long as you keep speaking in French.

Discussion is, of course, even more difficult to practise on your own! Again, if you have had a discussion in school, when you come home you should think about your part in the discussion and how you can improve it.

Did you contribute much to the discussion?
Did you have or take the opportunity to introduce an aspect?
Did you express an opinion?
Did you agree/disagree with someone?
Did you listen to what the other people were saying?

If you know that you are going to be taking part in a discussion, prepare in the following ways.

1. You will need to have the vocabulary and structures to express ideas. Consult your lists, and select those which are relevant to the topic you are to discuss. You will most likely be discussing an area related to the subject you are currently studying or have studied in the past.

   Decide what your attitude is going to be. Unlike a written essay you will not be expected to present a balanced view — though this should arise from the contributions made by everyone in the group. But note that your teacher may ask you to defend a view with which you do not agree in order to achieve a balance.

Remember you must give a reason for your opinion. It is not enough simply to agree.

*Je trouve le français vraiment intéressant **parce que** j'ai l'intention d'aller vivre au Canada.*

2. You will also have to have a good command of the structures necessary for any discussion. Which of the phrases used by each of the people in the drawing would be useful if you wanted to:
   - agree with someone
   - contradict someone
   - encourage someone else to speak
   - introduce a new point
   - persuade someone to think differently
   - express your own opinion
   - concede a point?

Collect other expressions as you meet them and add them to your vocabulary notebook. Here are some you probably know already. How would you use them?

- Moi aussi, je crois que. . .
- Mais tu oublies que. . .
- Je ne suis pas d'accord avec. . .
- Ah non, Martine/Martin. Tu as tort.

- Personnellement, je trouve que. . .
- Alain/Hélène a raison de dire que. . .
- Moi, je pense que. . .
- Jeanne/Jean a tort de dire que. . .

TASKS 👻

1. Open a discussion on:
   - le port de l'uniforme;
   - Noël;
   - les vacances en famille.

2. Agree with the following, giving a reason:
   - la discipline au collège est importante;
   - nous mangeons trop de chocolat, trop de bonbons;
   - on boit trop d'alcool en Ecosse.

3. Disagree with the following, giving a reason:
   - les teenagers ont trop d'argent de poche;
   - les jeunes passent trop de temps à regarder la télé;
   - nos parents ne nous comprennent pas.

4. Persuade someone to change their mind about:
   - nos profs sont trop sévères;
   - l'anglais, c'est ennuyeux;
   - la vie à la campagne est la meilleure espèce de vie.

Remember that in discussion you must make sure that you take an active part. If you don't say anything, or say very little, you cannot be given a good grade!

TESTS

Although there is no longer a Final Proficiency Speaking test set by the Examination Board for all candidates, your school may decide to set one test for the whole year group, either as part of your end of term examinations or nearer the time when the final grade is sent to the Board, about April in your fourth year.

Also, at some point towards the end of your course, a teacher from another school will perhaps come and hear you and some of your classmates carrying out a speaking activity. Do not be put off by this. The purpose of the visit is not really to 'examine' you, but to make sure that teachers all over the country are applying the same standards when they give candidates their grades.

The test itself is often set out as a conversation in which you will play yourself and your teacher will take the role of a French person, perhaps your exchange partner, your pen-friend's parent or someone you have met on holiday. You will be expected not only to make general conversation but to use the other speaking skills you have learned during your Standard Grade course.

In either of these test situations, or if you have smaller tests throughout the year as well as your class work, you will normally be given an outline of your test at least a day in advance. As soon as you have your copy, prepare for your test in the following way.

1. Read the question carefully.
   Make sure you know exactly what you are being asked to talk about. Read the outline two or three times. Notice the kind of structures you will need to be able to use. Look at this example.

Your exchange partner would like to see a bit more of Scotland during a visit. Talk about what you could do during the final weekend.

Be prepared, for example:
- to find out what kind of area your exchange partner would like to visit.
- to suggest places you think might be of interest.
- to discuss how you could travel and where to stay.
- to talk about a similar trip you have already made.

Your first reading should encourage you to think about the following:
- Your exchange partner — in this case you will have to remember to call your teacher (acting as the exchange partner) 'tu'.
- Talk about what you could do during the final weekend. Keep your suggestions practical. It is unlikely you could take your bikes and go 'island hopping', for example.
- Be prepared. Remember that these are suggestions which will help you plan what to say. You may be able to think of other areas which you could talk about within the same general situation. The more interested you and your partner become in the 'conversation', the less likely you are to stick rigidly to the set guidelines. This is fine . . . as long as you keep speaking in French.
- To find out what kind of area the partner would like to visit, ask questions: Où? Comment? As-tu visité. . .? Veux-tu. . .? Tu connais. . .?

- Suggest places you think might be of interest: On peut. . .? Si on. . .? Have alternatives ready in case your partner is not interested in some of them. Give information: Il y a. . . C'est très . . . etc.
- Discuss how you could travel and where to stay. Have several possibilities in mind. To be able to discuss a point you must look at the advantages and disadvantages of the matter. Express your opinion.
- Talk about a similar trip you have already made and use past tenses! Think of useful verbs: je suis allé(e), nous avons vu. . . c'était . . .

2. Copy out the instructions for the test in the centre of a blank piece of paper and underline the main vocabulary areas you will be required to cover. Use this to clarify your thoughts about what you will want to say. Leave plenty of room to add new ideas as they occur to you!

Remember the question!
Your exchange partner would like to see a bit more of Scotland during a visit. Talk about what you could do during the final weekend.

Be prepared, for example, to:

Tu connais..

Tu aimerais..

. . . **find out** what kind of area he/she would like to visit. . .

On peut..?

Si on..?

. . . **suggest** places you think might be of interest. . .

paysage magnifique

moi, je préfère..

. . . **discuss** how you could travel and where to stay. . .

parce que..

j'ai un cousin qui habite..

. . . **talk** about a similar trip you have already made. . .

la mer
↓
aller à la pêche   Largs ↖
la campagne   ↙
↓
la ferme de mon oncle ↖
                      ↙
site historique
hotel
↓
trop cher   ↖
- - - - - - - - -
camping   ↙
s'il pleut?

l'an dernier.. ←
il y a 3 ans.. ←
Quand j'avais 10 ans.. ↙
mes parents ont décidé..
mes copains et moi, nous sommes allés..

Aviemore {
les montagnes
↓
faire du ski
↓
Tu aimes ça?
}

Edinburgh {
une grande ville
↓
faire du shopping
↓
visiter les musées
}

↗ grands magasins
↘ un centre-loisirs

entrain / bus
↓
cher
↓
commode
- - - - - - - - -
à vélo
↓
s'il fait beau..
les bagages?

↗ On a visité..
↘ c'était vraiment ennuyeux.. super..

3. Revise any areas of vocabulary in which you feel weak, using your vocabulary notebooks and textbooks. The test will not usually include any subjects you have not (probably several times) covered in the time you have been learning French. So there should be no need to learn new phrases at this stage. Stick to those you feel confident with.

4. Practise your 'lines' out loud. You will not be allowed to use your notes during the test. After all, you are learning how to speak to people. If possible, work with a friend or a member of your family, taking turns to play both parts. Vary the suggestions you make, the kind of questions you ask and information you give each time. Pool your ideas and add them to your notes as you go along. If you are unable to see your friends after school, ask whoever pays the phone bill if on this occasion you can phone them to revise.

5. Practise without your notes. Put aside all your notes and books and try to think yourself into the situation. What **would** you show a visitor who wanted to see more of Scotland? Again try to do this with someone in your class, if possible.

6. On the day of the test, if it is not in normal class time, make sure you know where you are to go and be there in time to relax before your turn. Don't go over your notes again but do try to begin thinking in French before you start. Look around and think how you would describe what you see. If you have practised looking relaxed and confident during your classwork, smiling at the person you are speaking to and calling them by name, this should be quite natural to you now.

Make sure that you know phrases to use:
- if the other person speaks too quickly for you;
- if you wish a sentence to be repeated;
- if you have not understood what was said.

These phrases will stop the conversation drying up and show that you could ask for help in a real situation where you might have to speak French.

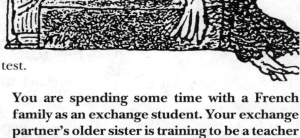

TASKS 👂

Prepare these situations as you would for a class test.

You have been spending a holiday with your pen-friend in Paris. You go to the travel agent's to make your travel arrangements to Calais to catch the ferry home.

Be prepared, for example, to:
- give the date and time of your crossing;
- find out how long the journey to Calais will take by train and bus and how much each would cost;
- discuss your preference with the travel agent and make your reservation;
- talk about yourself, where you come from and what you have been doing during your stay.

You are spending some time with a French family as an exchange student. Your exchange partner's older sister is training to be a teacher and talks to you about education in Scotland.

Be prepared, for example, to:
- describe the school you attend — the size, facilities and so on;
- talk about the subjects you take and how you feel about them;
- describe any after-school activities which are offered;
- find out what kind of school she attended and why she would like to be a teacher;
- discuss the school day in France and in Scotland.

CHAPTER FIVE

General Writing

In some ways the writing paper in Standard Grade French is unlike the other parts of the exam. There are only two sections — General and Credit. You sit the writing paper on a different day from the reading and listening tests, sometimes about one week later. It is very important for you to choose whether you want to sit it or not. If you do not, it will not influence your overall grade for French. Nor will your grade be affected if you do sit and do not do as well as you had hoped.

No doubt you will discuss your decision with your French teacher who will be able to give you advice based on your class work. You should also consider if a certificate which shows your ability to write in French might be useful for you later on. If you are hoping to continue with your French studies, say, to Higher or beyond, it is advisable to attempt the writing. This is also true if you are considering a career where you may have to take messages or write notes in French. In fact you should really only consider not sitting the writing paper if you are struggling to obtain the grades you want elsewhere in the paper and need the time to revise for those.

Like the speaking tasks, writing is your opportunity to show how well you can use French but as you will have more time to think out your answer, you should be more accurate in your use of the language.

You can use the same six steps we discussed in Chapter One to help you plan your revision here.

Use Your Time Wisely

If you have used previous papers for practice at home or in school, you will have noticed that you were given 30 minutes to complete five tasks. Since 1994 this has increased to 45 minutes in order to give you more time to plan your answers. You are normally asked to write about factual information 'to give and ask for straightforward information with some elaboration of basic statements'[1]. These are generally very short items, often three sentences in French, but it means that you have only about 9 minutes to think out, write down, and check each section.

It is important that you do not miss out any of the questions. Where five tasks have been set, you must succeed in communicating (in spite of errors) in four or five of the tasks to achieve a General Level award. The key phrase here is 'in spite of errors'. Your message may still be understood by a French person even though your answer is not 100% correct. However, the more accurate your answer, the better chance you have of a higher grade. A Grade 4 will be awarded for 'a satisfactory overall performance'; a Grade 3 for 'a high overall standard of performance'[2].

Think Ahead

Like the rest of the papers, most of your preparation for this section can been started well in advance of the exam day. Some you will have done since you started learning French when you made a note of new words and phrases.

The vocabulary notebook which you are using to help you revise for the speaking tasks is also part of your preparation for writing. In fact both skills can be revised at the same time, as the kind of tasks you are asked to perform are very similar. Check, however, that when you copy up new vocabulary you do so accurately — correct spelling (including accents!), nouns noted with gender (le or la) and useful phrases rather than single words.

As part of your revision, review any tasks you have completed in class and write out corrected versions. If you do not understand why something you have written is wrong, ask your teacher to explain. Otherwise you will continue to repeat the same kind of mistakes.

1 Scottish Examination Board — Revised Arrangements in French
2 Scottish Examination Board — Modern Languages on the Standard Grade: Guidance to Teachers on the Assessment of Writing at General and Credit Levels

There will be opportunities every day when you can practise writing French outside of the classroom. If you keep a diary the odd entry in French will hide your secrets from younger brothers and sisters. If those at home can read French, leave them notes when you go out telling them where you have gone and when you will be back.

You can also write out shopping lists, plans for the week ahead and notes to remind yourself of things to do. Of course, if you have a pen-friend in a French-speaking country, you will be writing at least some French in your letters to them.

Use Your Dictionary With Care

You are allowed to use a dictionary in the writing papers. But you should restrict this to checking gender and so on **after** you have decided what you are going to write. This is your opportunity to show what French you know, not to start learning new words and expressions. Most tasks should allow you to do this. If it is absolutely necessary for you to look up the English-French section to find a new word, try to avoid the common errors of using the wrong part of speech and choosing an inappropriate word.

SAY WHAT YOU MEAN. . .

You know that each word in your dictionary is preceded by an abbreviation which tells you whether it is a noun (*n*), verb (*v*), adjective (*adj*) or the like. Check which ones are used in the dictionary you will have on the day of the exam and learn to recognise them. They will help you decide which word to use.

What kind of word would you use to express the words in bold in each of the following? (Note: Don't look them up in the dictionary yet. For the moment we are only concerned with the kind of word, not with finding a French one.)

(a) to catch a **train**
    to **train** for a football match
(b) to **leave** the house
    the **leaves** are green
(c) **last** week
    to **last** a long time
(d) to **long** for the holidays
    to have **long** hair

Check your answers to this exercise in Chapter Eight before you go on to the next section.

▮ . . . AND MEAN WHAT YOU SAY

Once you have decided what kind of word you need, you will want to look it up in the dictionary. But not just yet! You know of course that in English we may use the same kind of word to express quite different ideas. A *bed* of flowers is nothing like the *bed* you sleep in. Someone who *runs* a

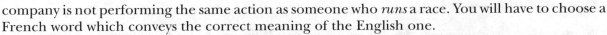

company is not performing the same action as someone who *runs* a race. You will have to choose a French word which conveys the correct meaning of the English one.

Your dictionary may help you pick the one which is appropriate for the idea you wish to express. For example you may read:

bed[bed] *n* lit m; *(of flowers)* parterre m; *(of coal, clay)* couche f;...

© Collins Gem French Dictionary 1991

The information given in brackets *(of flowers)* ... *(of coal, clay)* should help you avoid either 'parterre' or 'couche' as a suitable word for describing your bedroom. If you are still in doubt as to which word you need, you can check the entries for 'lit' in the French-English section. This may give you alternative English meanings which you can substitute without changing the sense of the sentence. Or there may be phrases illustrating the use of the French word.

It takes a long time to find and check just one word, including the time to look through the dictionary and read each entry — for example, even in quite a small dictionary 'run' takes about 58 lines and you will not have time on the exam day to check and double-check every word. So it is worth repeating that the dictionary is no substitute for learning the basic vocabulary you need by heart.

However, using a dictionary properly is a useful language skill to develop in class and at home. It is essential if you are to continue studying French beyond Standard Grade. You can practise just now by finding the most appropriate French word for each of the phrases we looked at earlier.

(a) to catch a **train**
    to **train** for a football match

(b) to **leave** the house
    the **leaves** are green

(c) **last** week
    to **last** a long time

(d) to **long** for the holidays
    to have **long** hair

Check your answers in Chapter Eight.

Read The Question Carefully/Select The Information You Need

Here, as in the other papers, it is essential that you answer the question which has been set. If you are asked to name **five** items, **four** will not do. If you are asked to describe what you **did**, you cannot answer in the present tense.

Your answer must be suitable to the task you have been given. Here are two similar questions.

TASK A

You are to meet your exchange partner at the train station. You have been asked to send a short description so that you can be recognised. Write at least three things about yourself in French.

TASK B

Your teacher is going to find pen-friends in France for your class and wants to match people with similar interests. Write at least three things in French about yourself.

Both tasks are asking for a description. In the first you would describe what you look like (hair, eyes, height...). In the second you must describe your interests (reading, cinema...). Remember that the examiner does not know you personally. Your S.C.E. exam will not be marked by your class teacher or anyone in your school. It is your use of French that is important here, not the absolute truth. If your eyes are bluish-green and you don't know how to say so, describe them as blue or green. (Of course, you will probably want to find this out for yourself by checking in the dictionary or by asking your class teacher **before** the exam.)

Check Your Answers

When you are writing a message for someone you will want to make your meaning as clear as possible. Unlike speaking you will not be there to explain what you meant to say. So you need to check over your work to correct any careless mistakes which might obscure your meaning.

Remember first of all that you are writing to communicate with a French person. So there is no point in writing down English words to pad out your answer. If you can't say it in French, miss it out or write something else.

Secondly, check that you have not missed out words or phrases which are necessary to convey your meaning. Try reading your answer out loud — in your head if you are in a class or exam room! A series of phrases may not make much sense if a vital verb is missing. If you are giving directions, have you included the prepositions which tell someone if it is near, to the right of or behind the cinema?

When you read over your class work you may find that, in spite of your best efforts, you have repeated the same kind of language error — wrong verb agreement, wrong gender, spelling — so check over your answer for whatever you know is your weakness. If more than one, check for each one separately.

On the following pages you will find examples of the kind of tasks you can expect to find in the General writing paper, along with some hints on how you can improve your work by paying attention to dictionary and grammar skills.

GIVING INFORMATION

You may, for example, be asked to write a few sentences about your home town or what you like to eat and drink. You should have the vocabulary for this kind of exercise at your fingertips before you go into the exam room. In order to check your work you must also bear in mind the grammar rules you have learned in class.

As you know, where we use one word 'the' (called the definite article) there are **four** words in French. Here is the rule to remind you.

	singular	before a vowel	plural
with masculine nouns	**le** château	**l'**aéroport	**les** magasins
with feminine nouns	**la** cathédrale	**l'**école	**les** boutiques

You may wish to write about a type of article (**a** swimming pool rather than **the** swimming pool); some of certain items (**some** coffee not **the** coffee); or a quantity (**a jar of** coffee). Again, the correct word to use for **a** (known as the indefinite article) or **some** will depend on whether the noun is masculine or feminine.

A and an become:

	singular	plural
with masculine nouns	**un** château	**des** magasins
with feminine nouns	**une** cathédrale	**des** boutiques

Some and any become:

	singular	before a vowel	plural
with masculine nouns	**du** café	**de l'**huile	**des** légumes
with feminine nouns	**de la** crème	**de l'**eau	**des** pommes

Remember that **'some'** is often omitted in English but never in French:
I'd like oranges and pears = Je voudrais **des** oranges et **des** poires.

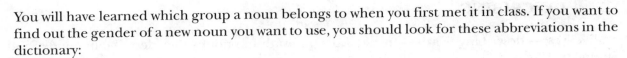

You will have learned which group a noun belongs to when you first met it in class. If you want to find out the gender of a new noun you want to use, you should look for these abbreviations in the dictionary:

nm = masculine noun; *nf* = feminine noun.

Remembering whether a noun is masculine or feminine when you learn what it means will help you to be more accurate in your writing and in your speaking. It may even make a difference to the meaning of the word. Do you know the difference between: **le tour** and **la tour**? — **le livre** and **la livre**? If not, use your dictionary to find out now. Then check in Chapter Eight.

TASK ✍

Suppose you had written the following information about where you live. Can you complete the blanks with the correct words for 'the' without using the dictionary?

Ma ville se trouve dans . . . sud de . . . Écosse.
. . . cathédrale et . . . musées sont très célèbres.
Mais moi, je préfère . . . stade et . . . piscine.

Check your answers in Chapter Eight.

TASK ✍

Choose another town — perhaps the area where you live or where you have been on holiday. Write three sentences about this town.

These need not be about famous buildings, but might include information on the park(s), the swimming pool, theatres. In the exam you will want to stick to the ordinary places in a town, words which you know well from class. You might be interested now, however, to find out the French names for any more unusual places in your area, for example: the abbey, the distillery, the wildlife park or the glass factory. If you look these up in the dictionary, remember to cross-check them in the French section for any ambiguous meanings. It is always a good idea to check with a native French speaker, like the foreign assistant if your school has one, to make sure that you have a correct translation.

In French remember that **le**, **la**, **l'** and **les** are also used where the noun has a general sense in a way that we do not use terms in our own language.

J'aime **le** café = I like coffee (i.e. coffee in general not a particular kind).
Je n'aime pas **les** bananes = I don't like bananas.

You should know by heart a few examples of what you like to eat and drink, or your favourite hobbies, etc. You will have revised these already for speaking tests, so all you need to do is check over your spelling.

TASK ✍

Your exchange class wants to compare the interests of pupils in your class with those of pupils in France. They have asked you to fill in a questionnaire. Try to write three sentences in answer to each question below. For example: Quel est ton animal préféré?
J'adore les chiens. Ils sont plus sympa que les chats. Ils sont aussi plus intelligents!

Quelle est ta saison favorite?   Quelle est ta matière favorite?
Quel est ton sport favori?   Quelles sont tes vacances préférées?

 DESCRIBING

Adjectives — describing words — must also agree with the nouns they describe in gender and number.

	singular	plural
masculine nouns	un manteau noir	des tee-shirts bleu**s**
feminine nouns	une jupe vert**e**	des sandales brun**es**

These are very simple descriptions and you will know many other phrases like 'en coton' or 'rayé' to make it more interesting.

TASKS ✍

Revise the adjectives you know now and write a short description of:
1. what you wear at the weekend;
2. what you wear to school;
3. your ideal school uniform.

To describe a person, you should revise the set phrases you know which convey what a person looks like.

For yourself, these will all begin with 'je':

Je suis assez grande. ('grand' if you are a boy)
J'ai les yeux bleus et les cheveux noirs.

If describing a female, e.g. your mother, you use 'elle' and the adjectives will agree.

Elle est assez petite et très jolie.
Elle a les yeux verts et les cheveux courts et blancs.

If describing a male, e.g. your brother, you use 'il':

Il est très petit et mince.
Il porte des lunettes.
Il a les yeux marron et les cheveux bruns.

You may also wish to mention your own or someone else's character.

Je suis assez timide.
Ma sœur est très sympa.
Mon père est assez sévère.

TASKS ✍

1. Write a description of yourself 30 years from now.
2. Choose **two** famous pop stars, politicians or television personalities (one male and one female). Write a description of each and give it to someone in your class to guess who it is.
3. Describe someone in your class or your teacher *from memory*. Next time you see that person check how many details you got right.

Remember that you must read the whole question. You may be asked for two (or more) points of information. You must then complete all parts to fulfil the task.
    Try the next three tasks for practice.

TASKS ✍

1. Your exchange partner has written to ask you about the school day in Scotland.
   Write a note in which you explain: what time the classes begin;
   how many lessons there are each day;
   how long the lunch hour lasts.

   There may be suggestions about what you can write. Here you need not stick to the set questions but you should stick to the main theme of the assignment.

2. Your pen-friend has asked you about your plans for your birthday.
   Write at least **three** sentences.
   You could say, for example: what presents you would like;
   what you are going to have to eat and drink;
   what you plan to do that day.

   Notice that in the last section you are asked what you plan **to do**. After you have checked the nouns and adjectives in your answer, you should then read over the verbs you have used, making sure you have used the correct tense as well as the person.

3. Write three things about: what you normally do on Saturdays;
   what you did last Saturday;
   what you are going to do next Saturday.

   Check the verbs in each sentence.

A very useful verb here is 'faire' = to make or do, which is used in many set phrases. Can you match the French with its translation in the next column?

faire la vaisselle	to go for a picnic
faire une promenade	to go shopping
faire le jardin	to make the beds
faire des courses	to make some coffee
faire un pique-nique	to do the garden
faire les lits	to do the washing up
faire du café	to go for a walk

> **Remember also the verbs:**
> aller = to go
> jouer (au football, au tennis etc.) = to play
> visiter = to visit places
> voir = to see

▮▮ GIVING INSTRUCTIONS

You will often have heard your teacher giving instructions to the class in French.

    Écoutez!   Finissez cet exercice!   Attendez!

Your teacher will also have spoken to you as an individual.

    Écoute!   Finis cet exercice!   Attends!

You know that the first form (Écoutez! Finissez! Attendez!) is from the 'vous' part of the verb and is used when speaking to a group of people or someone you would address **formally** — you would call them Mr Smith or Mrs Smith rather than John or Jane.

The second (Écoute! Regarde! Lis!) is used when speaking **informally** to friends or relatives — that is people you would address by their first name. This is taken from the 'tu' part of the verb and you will remember that when the verb belongs to the -er conjugation and with 'aller' you drop the 's' of that ending so:

Tu vas = you go   Va! = Go!
Tu parles = you speak   Parle! = Speak!

This single word form of the verb is very effective when you want to attract someone's attention, but it can be a rather abrupt way of giving a command or instruction. Just as in English, you can sound more polite by using the full form of the verb

Monte cette rue! — Go up this street! Tu montes cette rue. — You go up this street.
Montez cette rue! — Go up this street! Vous montez cette rue. — You go up this street.

Using the infinitive of the verb after 'Il faut' (you must — used for both tu and vous) or Tu devrais/Vous devriez (you should) will also make your instructions sound less blunt.

Il faut monter cette rue = You must go up this street.

Tu devrais
Vous devriez } monter cette rue.   You should go up this street.

Sometimes you will want to tell someone what **not** to do, that is, in French you will use **ne . . . pas**, for example:

Tu ne devrais pas monter cette rue. You should not go up this street.

TASKS ✍

1. Your pen-friend is spending a week's holiday at your house and has asked for some ideas on how to help in the house. Write out a list of suggestions.
2. What rules would you have in an ideal school? Make up your own list.
3. A young French child is staying with you during the Easter holidays. You have been asked to hide some Easter eggs throughout the house. Write a series of simple clues to help your visitor find them.

Bear in mind that you may wish to include information as well as instructions. For example, if you were asked to write a note telling someone how to get from your house to the shops, you might include the times of buses and which number to get as well as how to get to the bus stop and where to get off.

ASKING FOR INFORMATION

What kind of questions would you ask if you had to write an interview with the French assistant for the school magazine, or if you were interviewing an exchange pupil?

Again the form of the question would depend on whether you called the person 'vous' (as with the assistant) or 'tu' (with someone of your own age). The content of the question would depend on what you wanted to know. You might wish to begin with some general personal questions of the kind you will have practised frequently in class.

Here are some personal questions written in the 'vous' form. Write them out again in the 'tu' form. Remember to check the spelling of the verbs before you look at the answers in Chapter Eight.

(a) Comment vous appelez-vous?
(b) Quel âge avez-vous?

(c) D'où venez-vous?

(d) Vous êtes français? (française for a female)

(e) Vous avez des frères ou des sœurs?

(f) Avez-vous des animaux à la maison?

The last three are of course the simplest way to ask questions. In (d) and (e) you simply add a question mark to a statement. In (f) the verb has been turned around. You will also want to asks questions like those in (a) to (c) where you use a specific question word.

Do you remember these...?	
Qui?	(a) . . . se trouve ton collège?
Où?	(b) . . . y vas-tu?
Combien?	(c) Avec . . . y vas-tu?
Comment?	(d) . . . les cours commencent-ils?
A quelle heure?	(e) . . . de leçons as-tu par jour?
Quel? (quelle? quels? quelles?)	(f) . . . est ta matière préférée?
Qu'est-ce que?	(g) . . . l'aimes-tu?
Pourquoi?	(h) . . . tu fais le soir?

Which of the question words on the left would make most sense in the questions which you might ask about your pen-friend's school?

TASKS ✍

1. You will be spending a holiday as a guest with a French family. They have asked you to send them a note of any questions you want to ask about your stay. Write down some questions:
    * about the area in which they live;
    * about the members of the family;
    * about their house;
    * about the weather, what clothes to bring and anything else you think you would need to know.

2. You have the chance to interview Gérard Depardieu/Alain Prost/Vanessa Paradis for your school magazine. What questions would you ask?

▮▮ LEAVING MESSAGES

You may wish to leave a note for a French-speaking guest, or for your hosts if you are in France, telling them that you have gone out and when you will be back. Or you may be asked to pass on a message you have taken down on the phone and you write it down so you do not forget. Remember that you will have to give *all* the information required as accurately as possible. Pay careful attention to the tense you are required to use to avoid confusion. For example:

I have gone = Je suis allée (allé if you are a boy)...

I am going to go = Je vais aller...

Remember, too, that expressions of what will happen in the future may be expressed in the present tense in French:

Je reviens à/vers/avant/après . . . = I will come back at/about/before/after

Your verb must not only convey the time of the event but must also agree with the person or object you are writing about:

> Ton père est allé . . ./Ta mère est allée . . .
> Il va aller. . ./Elle va aller. . .
> Il revient. . ./Elle revient. . .

TASK ✐

You will be spending a week with a French family. Write a short note telling them how and when you are travelling and when you hope to arrive.

◼◻ DESCRIBING EVENTS

If you have a French-speaking pen-friend, you will no doubt include descriptions in your letters of where you have been and what you have been doing. In the exam, too, you will be expected to write a few sentences describing events which have taken place. You may write a diary during your visit noting what you have done each day. Or you may be asked to write a thank you note to your hosts and describe your journey home. Again you must read the question carefully and use the appropriate tense.

TASK ✐

Here are some of the verbs you might need to describe events in the past. Finish each one to make a sensible sentence.

Je suis allé(e). . .	J'ai joué. . .
Je suis arrivé(e). . .	J'ai vu. . .
J'ai visité. . .	J'ai fait. . .

Can you think of any other verbs you might need? Do you know the form of each of them in the perfect? Remember that although your dictionary will probably have a list of irregular verbs, this will be of little use unless you know how to form the perfect tense. You will have a note in your grammar book or from your teacher to revise if you have forgotten.

If you keep a diary for a week in French — noting down each evening where you have been, what you have seen and what you have done — you will notice the kind of verbs which you need most often.

It is also worthwhile to remember the phrase 'C'était. . .' = It was, if you want to describe what something **was** like:

> C'était super! C'était moche! C'était intéressant! C'était ennuyeux!
> C'était amusant! C'était bête! C'était formidable! C'était cher!

TASK ✐

Use one of the phrases above, or another one you know well, to describe each of the events in the previous exercise.

Once again the remainder of this chapter consists of two tests, each very similar to the exam. For each test chose a time when you can work undisturbed for 45 minutes and you feel quite fresh. Take note of how long you take to do each one.

Tackle each test the way you will in the exam, using the techniques you have practised in this chapter and allocating your time wisely.

TEST 1

Write your answers in FRENCH. You may use a French dictionary.

> *Use your time wisely.*   *Read the question carefully.*
> *Think ahead.*   *Select the information you need.*
> *Use your dictionary with care.*   *Check your answers.*

You will be spending part of your holidays with your French pen-friend Isabelle in the town of Bordeaux.

1. You decide to write to the *Syndicat d'Initiative* in advance to ask for some information about Bordeaux.
   Write at least **three** sentences.
   You could ask, for example, if they have a leaflet about the town;
   what leisure facilities are available;
   what the weather is like.

2. Isabelle's parents will be meeting you at the station.
   Write a note in which you:
   — tell them when you will arrive in Bordeaux;
   — suggest where you can meet at the station;
   — tell them you will have something to eat on the train.

3. During your visit, Isabelle's young brother asks you to help him with his geography project about Scotland.
   Write at least **three** sentences about your home town.
   You could say, for example, where it is;
   what kind of area it is;
   whether you like living there.

4. You notice a questionnaire in a magazine asking what teenagers do in their free time. You decide to fill it in.
   Mention any **three** things about your hobbies.

5. When you return to Scotland you write a postcard to your hosts, thanking them for your visit and describing your journey home. Mention any **three** things about your journey.

TEST 2

Write your answers in FRENCH. You may use a French dictionary.

> *Use your time wisely.*
> *Think ahead.*
> *Use your dictionary with care.*
>
> *Read the question carefully.*
> *Select the information you need.*
> *Check your answers.*

As part of an exchange programme a group of young French people will be visiting your school for a month. One of the students will be staying with you.

Write a few words in **French** for each of the following items. You may use a French dictionary.

1. The French students have written to ask what there is to do and see in the area.
   Write **three** suggestions.

2. Your class wishes to know a bit more about the French teenagers. Make up a short question-naire to send them.
   Ask at least **three** questions.

3. Your exchange student will be spending some time in your school and has written to ask you for more details.
   You could mention, for example, what you usually wear to school;
   what school equipment is needed;
   what time you get up in the morning.

4. Your exchange student arrives but has a minor accident at school. You take him/her to hospital.
   Write a short note to the teacher explaining what has happened, where you have gone and when you will be back.

5. You keep in touch with your exchange student by writing to each other after the visit.
   Write at least **three** sentences to describe what you did to celebrate when your exams were finally over!

CHAPTER SIX

Credit Writing

There is a very great difference between the tasks set at General Level and the one task set at Credit Level. Instead of writing four or five sentences about five different items, you now have to write about 200 words on one topic. You will need to have a wide range of vocabulary and structures at your disposal, as well as a sound knowledge of grammar if you are going to be able to do this. It is important that you start your preparation for the Writing paper well in advance of the examination, so that you have ample time to build up your resources. Just because the writing papers are optional, it does not mean that preparation for them should be tackled as an afterthought. There is a similarity between Speaking and Writing and you should aim to improve your performance in both at the same time.

The Writing paper will present you with a number of very short French passages giving the views of some people on a particular topic. There will also be some questions in English on the topic to guide you to express your own views. You will be required to state some facts about the topic and to indicate your opinions and feelings about it. It is unlikely that the general subject will be one that you have not covered in school — the most common topics are holidays and leisure, school, career, family life, relationships with teachers, parents, friends and so on — but the aspect to be considered may be somewhat different, so make sure you do not reproduce in its entirety an essay you have learned by heart, as it may be irrelevant to the guideline questions set in the examination. Once again the first step will be to read the questions carefully.

To prepare yourself for this exercise, you should collect useful vocabulary and phrases under topic headings, — e.g. leisure, with subtopics of television, pop music, sport and any others you can think of. Add to these lists as you meet new words, for example in Reading passages. Test yourself from time to time.

Also, you should aim to build up your command of structures which can be used in any essay. Here is an example: you are writing an essay on television and state **'Je passe des heures à** regarder la télé.' Then you come to write an essay on what you do on holiday. You use the same structure and say **'Je passe des heures à** me bronzer au soleil.' Similarly, in the television essay, you express the opinion, **'Je trouve** les documentaires **très intéressants**'. You come to the holiday essay and say **'Je trouve** les vacances à la campagne **très ennuyeuses**'.

To make your essay read well, you should also have a number of joining words or introductory words at your disposal, such as 'First of all, I. . .' (**'D'abord, je. . .'**), 'On the other hand,. . .' (**'Par contre,. . .'**), 'As far as I am concerned,. . .' (**'Pour moi,. . .'**) and so on. You should compile a list of these expressions as you go along. To summarise the above:

- Start your preparation early on in the session.
- Collect vocabulary and structures under topic headings.
- Collect useful structures, including expressions of feelings and opinions.
- Collect phrases to help you link the different parts of your essay.

Pay particular attention to the grammar which you are being taught in school, especially the verbs, and ask your teacher to explain to you anything about which you are in doubt.

The advice which you are given on using the dictionary in the General Writing section applies to Credit also. However, in Credit, you may find that you want to check the meanings of some of the French words in the short passages. You should then follow the advice given under Reading in Chapter Three — you do not need to look up every word and you should be trying to work out the meaning of any words you feel you really need to understand as you look them up.

This chapter is divided into two sections. The first section aims to help you to draw useful information, vocabulary and structures from short French passages. This is the kind of exercise you can practise in class and while doing your normal homework to build up your resources for the Writing test. The second section will look more closely at technique on the day of the examination.

TASK 1 ✎

1. Read quickly through these short statements and write down in French what the topic is.

   Some young French people answer a question about sport.

Pratiquez-vous un sport?

L'équitation est pour moi une passion: elle occupe la première place dans ma vie, car cela m'apprend à 'communiquer' avec le cheval. **Camille**

Moi, je fais de la danse et du volleyball, ce qui est tout à fait différent. Quand je danse, tout ce que j'ai fait à l'école, chez moi, et tout ce qui se passe en dehors, je l'oublie, je ne pense à rien. **Séverine**

J'adore le sport! Il me permet de m'amuser et de me détendre, tout en gardant la forme. Pour moi, l'athlétisme, plus précisément le cross, est une passion. **Cécile**

Le sport est un élément essentiel à la vie, au bon fonctionnement du corps, aussi bien physiquement que moralement. Le basket est un jeu collectif qui apprend à être ordonné. Le tennis, qui est un sport individuel, développe la concentration. **Charles**

Pour moi, le sport prend une place importante dans ma vie, car je fais environ 10 heures de sport par semaine. Je fais du football et du handball, plus le sport pratiqué au collège. **Frédéric**

Adapted from *Okapi*, 15–28 février 1993

---

2. Read the passages again and make a list in French of all the sports mentioned (including the article — **le**, **la** or **l'**).

3. Write down in French (in the infinitive form):
   (a) to go in for/have a sport
   (b) to dance and play volleyball
   (c) to play football and handball.

   Note the structures you have used in (b) and (c) and write down how you would say:
   (d) to play basketball and tennis
   (e) to go horse-riding and take part in athletics.

4. Note that with **games** you can also use the structure 'jouer au' (football, tennis etc.).

   Check your answers in Chapter Eight.

Usually when you are writing your composition you will, like the young French people here, be writing about what **you** do, and the subject will very often be **je**, but this will not always be the case. It is not enough for you to be able to say 'je fais de l'athlétisme', but you also must be able to say what you do with your friends, using **on** or **nous**, to say what a friend does, using **il** or **elle**, or to say what a number of your friends do using **ils** or **elles**. You will not be able, at this level, to rely entirely on phrases you have learned, but you will have to show that you can be flexible and adapt such phrases to various situations. In other words, you will have to be able to use verbs accurately. At the moment, we are concerned with the present tense. You must be familiar, at the very least, with the regular families of verbs — the **-er** verbs, like jouer and regarder; the **-ir** verbs like choisir and finir, and the **-re** verbs like répondre and attendre, together with with a number of very common irregular verbs like:

être	avoir	aller	faire	dire
voir	mettre	prendre	devoir	pouvoir
vouloir	croire	connaître	savoir	venir

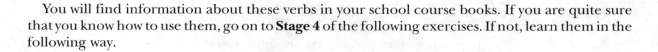

You will find information about these verbs in your school course books. If you are quite sure that you know how to use them, go on to **Stage 4** of the following exercises. If not, learn them in the following way.

Stage 1

Copy out the present tense in full of one or two verbs, underlining the endings..

Stage 2 (next day)

See if you can write them out from memory. If you cannot, copy them again and try to memorise them. If you can, go on to:

Stage 3

Put the subject pronouns in jumbled order, e.g.

il. . .	vous. . .	on. . .
nous. . .	je. . .	ils. . .
tu. . .	elles. . .	elle. . .

and fill in the appropriate parts of the verbs you have learned. Check your answers. Repeat this process, until you are confident in using all the verbs you think you will want to use. Once you have practised all the verbs mentioned above, try the following exercise to see how accurate you are.

Stage 4

Replace the infinitive by the correct form of the present tense of the verb in the following paragraph.

> Moi, je (faire) de l'athlétisme, et je (jouer) au tennis avec mes amies. Mon frère (faire) du handball au collège et pendant les vacances nous (faire) de l'équitation ensemble. Dans ma classe, les garçons (jouer) au football tous les mercredis et les filles (faire) du volleyball. Et toi, qu'est-ce que tu (faire) comme sport? Tu (jouer) au basket peut-être?

Check your answers in Chapter Eight, then decide how much practice you need with the present tense of verbs.

Now look at the above paragraph and note that in some cases it has been stated **who** you play with (avec mes amies), **where** you play (au collège) and **when** you play (pendant les vacances, tous les mercredis). This helps to avoid having too many very short sentences. Choose three activities that you (or your friends) take part in and write a short paragraph about them.

Remember that what you write doesn't need to be true! If you really are not interested in sport yourself, and don't want to pretend you are, write the paragraph about other people (ma sœur, mon frère, mes ami(e)s etc.). Sometimes you could use the structure **jouer au** and sometimes **faire du/de l'** to give some variety. Expand your sentences by telling us **who**, **where** and **when**.

When you have finished your paragraph, check it in the following way; one thing at a time.
- Check all plural nouns and adjectives to see that they have a plural ending (s or x).
- Check all words for accents.
- Check all genders: le, la, mon, ma etc.
- Check all verb endings. Do they agree with their subjects?

Now add the names of any sports which you did not know to your **leisure** vocabulary list, and add any useful structures in the texts to your useful phrases and structures collection.

TASK 2 ✍

In the Credit Level Writing Paper, as well as writing about what you do, you will be asked to state your opinions. This exercise should help you to build up a stock of useful structures to help you express your views.

1. Read the views of the young French people and write down in French the subject they are examining.

   Some young people express their views on video games.

Les jeux vidéo sont mon principal loisir. Je trouve que c'est un bon moyen de se divertir, mais il ne faut pas en abuser.
Igor

Je pense que les jeux électroniques sont utiles dans notre vie, ils nous occupent et peuvent distraire, mais il ne faut pas dépasser les limites, c'est-à-dire en devenir malade.
Marie

Je crois que les jeux de combats pourraient conduire à la violence. Mais certains jeux peuvent instruire les enfants, c'est quand même important. Pour ma part, les jeux électroniques ne prennent pas une grande place dans ma vie.
Florient

Je suis convaincu que tous ces jeux Sega, Nintendo, sont complètement idiots. Je suis sûr qu'ils peuvent nous faire mal, nous abîmer les yeux par exemple.
Jean-Pierre

Les jeux électroniques prennent une place importante dans ma vie. Parfois je commence un jeu et, une ou deux heures plus tard, j'y suis encore. Mais cela fait du bien, de temps en temps, d'en faire. Cela détend les nerfs.
Lucile

Adapted from *Okapi*, 15–30 juin 1993

---

2. Igor uses the expression 'Je trouve que...' to introduce his opinion. Write down:
   (a) how Marie does it
   (b) how Florient does it and
   (c) how Jean-Pierre does it. (2 ways)

3. Write down in French *three* of the advantages mentioned and *two* of the disadvantages — or more, if you can find them!

4. Note how Florient said that the games were not very important in his life, and how Lucile said they were in hers.

5. Find the French for: (a) that is   (b) all the same   (c) as far as I'm concerned.

   Check your answers in Chapter Eight.

You should now write a short paragraph expressing your own views on this topic. Begin by writing a general statement 'Les jeux électroniques . . . dans ma vie.' Then write a few sentences backing up this statement, that is, if they are important to you, write about their advantages, if not, state some of the disadvantages. The vocabulary you have noted above will help you, but of course you can also use any other relevant vocabulary and phrases you have met at school. You could write something putting a different point of view (Il est vrai que...) before coming back to making a final statement of your own attitude.

   Now take television as a topic and write a similar paragraph expressing your opinion, with advantages and disadvantages.

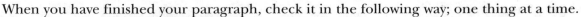

When you have finished your paragraph, check it in the following way; one thing at a time.
- Check all plural nouns and adjectives to see that they have a plural ending (s or x).
- Check all words for accents.
- Check all genders: le, la, mon, ma etc.
- Check all verb endings. Do they agree with their subjects?

Add any new vocabulary and structures to your lists.

TASK 3 ✍

1. Read quickly through the statements made and write down in French what the topic is.

In the following short texts, some young French people tell us how they feel about life in the country and in the town.

Que pensez-vous de la campagne?

J'aime la campagne plus que la ville. Je fais ce choix car la campagne est calme, moins polluée que la ville, très verte: on y a plus de place. Pour moi, la campagne, c'est le paradis sur terre. Mais, quand même, il y a beaucoup de choses intéressantes à faire en ville. **Joëlle**

Moi, j'habite à la campagne, mais je vais bientôt déménager pour la ville. Personnellement, je trouve que les deux ont des avantages. La campagne, c'est sympa: la ferme, les animaux etc. La ville, d'un autre côté, c'est pratique: le collège juste à côté; les bus; on peut plus souvent sortir avec des amis, pratiquer des sports etc. **Pierre**

La campagne, c'est moins pollué que la ville, on respire mieux; et puis les gens sont moins froids, moins agressifs. C'est sûr, on est plus loin des grandes surfaces*, où les choses sont souvent moins chères. Moi, j'habite dans un coin retiré de la ville, c'est presque la campagne. Et c'est silencieux. En un mot, c'est génial. **Muriel**

Je n'aime pas beaucoup la campagne. Elle signifie, pour moi, l'isolement et l'ennui. La ville, elle, est un endroit sympa pour se divertir. Entre les magasins, le cinéma, la piscine, on s'ennuie jamais. Cependant, la campagne est un endroit agréable pour se balader à vélo, sans se faire renverser par une voiture. **Astrid**

En fait, j'habite à la fois en ville et à la campagne. Ma maison est juste à côté des champs et, à un kilomètre à peine, il y a la ville. Je trouve qu'habiter à la campagne, c'est vraiment génial. Quant à la ville, je trouve que c'est très agréable. J'adore faire du lèche-vitrine, flâner dans les rues piétonnières ou arpenter les avenues. **Cécile**

*grandes surfaces = hypermarchés

Adapted from *Okapi*, 15–31 août 1992

---

2. Write down in French at least three advantages which the writers find in life:
   (a) in the country   (b) in the town.

3. In **Task 2**, you learned several ways of expressing your opinions. (Je trouve que, je pense que, etc.) This time you are going to look for some ways of saying how you **feel** about things. Make a list of the ways in which these young people say they **like** the country or the town.

4. Look at Cécile's statement and write down how you say:
   (a) in (the) town   (b) in the country

5. Find the French for the following expressions:
   (a) for me/as far as I'm concerned

(b) all the same
(c) personally
(d) on the other hand
(e) in a word
(f) yet
(g) in (actual) fact
(h) as for (the town)

Check your answers in Chapter Eight.

You should now be ready to express your own feelings about country/town life. Take time to plan what you are going to say. You could begin by saying where you live and making a general statement about whether you like it or not. Notice that Pierre and Muriel both used the structure '**Moi**, j'habite. . .'. This makes it more emphatic and catches the attention of the reader. As was stated in Task 2, you should now go on to back up your first statement, using the phrases you have noted above and any others which you know. Remember to say what you feel about things from time to time and also what you think. You will see that Pierre in his statement says 'on peut souvent sortir avec des amis, pratiquer des sports.' You can give some personal examples of these activities (e.g. 'chaque samedi, je vais. . .' or 'je joue au. . .'). Astrid and Cécile also suggest some activities. You could now consider some advantages of the other place to live, before stating which you really prefer. (Notice how Muriel finishes off her statement.)

When you have finished, check your work in the following way; one thing at a time.
- Check all plural nouns and adjectives to see that they have a plural ending (s or x).
- Check all words for accents.
- Check all genders: le, la, mon, ma etc.
- Check all verb endings. Do they agree with their subjects?

Add any new vocabulary, structures and useful joining phrases to your lists.

TASK 4 ✍

In these extracts, some French teenagers are talking about countries they would like to visit.

Dans quel pays partiriez-vous?

Moi, le pays où je voudrais vivre serait la Grèce. Surtout pour la chaleur, les îles, les maisons blanches, les beaux rochers. Mais j'adore aussi la manière de vivre des habitants, car il y a beaucoup de sympathie entre les gens.   *Elodie*

Moi, ce serait en Inde ou bien au Népal que j'irais. Ces deux pays me passionnent, et cela fait maintenant longtemps que j'aimerais y aller.   *Claire*

C'est vrai que le choix est dur, mais, moi, j'aimerais aller en Australie. Je ferais un safari là-bas, pour voir les kangourous, les koalas, les émeus. . .   *Paul*

Je crois que si j'avais le choix, je choisirais de partir aux Etats-Unis, car, là-bas, il y a beaucoup de cultures différentes.   *Stéphanie*

Si l'on m'offrait un voyage, sans hésiter, je choisirais un pays du tiers monde, le Bangladesh, l'Ethiopie. . . Des êtres humains meurent, chaque jour, de faim ou de maladie, donc mon voyage aurait un but humanitaire.   *Anne*

Adapted from *Okapi*, 1–15 septembre 1992

---

1. Complete the following statements, remembering what you have already learned about countries, i.e. that you say **en** with feminine countries and **au** with masculine.

Elodie aimerait aller . . . .

Claire aimerait aller . . . . ou . . . .

Paul aimerait aller . . . .

Stéphanie aimerait aller . . . .

Anne aimerait aller . . . . ou . . . .

2. Now find the French for:
   (a) the country where I would like to live
   (b) would be Greece
   (c) it would be to India or Nepal
   (d) that I would go
   (e) I would like to go to Australia
   (f) I would go on safari
   (g) I would choose to go to the U.S.A.
   (h) my journey would have a humanitarian purpose.

   Check your answers in Chapter Eight.

3. Underline all the verbs in question 2 above. They are all in a tense which we call the **conditional** tense which is most often expressed in English by the word 'would'. To make this tense, the rule is to add the endings -ais, -ais,-ait, -ions, -iez, -aient to the infinitive of the verb.
   Here is the conditional tense of the verb regarder in full:

je regarder**ais**	nous regarder**ions**
tu regarder**ais**	vous regarder**iez**
il regarder**ait**	ils regarder**aient**

   Of course there are always some exceptions to this rule and with some verbs you just have to learn what it is you have to add the endings to!
   Find the **je** form of the conditional tense of the following verbs from question 2 and write them down:

   aimer　　　**aller**　　　**avoir**　　　**choisir**　　　**être**　　　**faire**　　　**vouloir**

   Look at the verb tables in your school course book or your dictionary and again write the **je** form of the conditional tense of:

   attendre　　　**connaître**　　　**croire**　　　**devoir**　　　**dire**　　　**mettre**
   pouvoir　　　**prendre**　　　**savoir**　　　**venir**　　　**voir**

4. Now write a short paragraph about your ideal place to live. Use the conditional tense to say in what country it would be (town or country or seaside), what the climate would be like, what you would do there — but of course you may also use the present tense to explain why you would like to live there (j'adore la chaleur etc.).
   When you have finished, check your work in the following way; one thing at a time.
   • Check all plural nouns and adjectives to see that they have a plural ending (s or x).
   • Check all words for accents.
   • Check all genders: le, la, mon, ma etc.
   • Check all verb endings. Do they agree with their subjects?

5. Look at the following sentence: 'si j'avais le choix, je choisirais de partir aux Etats-Unis.'
   We have already seen that 'je choisirais de partir' means 'I would choose to go'. The first part of the sentence sets the situation for us — if I **had** the choice. Notice that the verb in the 'if' clause is in the imperfect tense, a tense which has the same endings as the conditional tense, but these endings are added to the stem of the verb, not to the infinitive. (The imperfect tense of 'regarder' is 'je regardais'.)

Complete the following sentences in any sensible way, using phrases you already know (about holidays, leisure activities etc.).

Si j'avais beaucoup d'argent, je ....

Si j'avais beaucoup de temps libre, je ....

Si j'avais le choix, je ....

Si j'étais à sa place, je ....

Si je n'avais pas de télé, je ....

Si j'étais directeur/directrice de mon collège, je ....

6. Now select one of the above sentences and write a short paragraph, telling us more things you would do if you were in that situation.

   When you have finished, check your work in the following way; one thing at a time.

   • Check all plural nouns and adjectives to see that they have a plural ending (s or x).

   • Check all words for accents.

   • Check all genders: le, la, mon, ma etc.

   • Check all verb endings. Do they agree with their subjects?

Add any new vocabulary and useful structures to your lists.

TASK 5 ✍

1. Write down, in French, the subject of the following statements.

Some young French people give their views on the environment.

L'écologie

Personnellement, je pense que la protection de la planète est vitale pour nous, et que, sans les forêts, l'ozone et l'air pur, notre vie est perdue. Chez moi, on récupère le verre, les piles, pour les recycler. Lorsque mes amis jettent des ordures et des papiers par terre, je leur demande de les ramasser.
                                                                                                            Henri

Je suis fière de dire que je suis une écolo! J'ai influencé mes parents, ma famille et des amis: maintenant, ensemble, nous achetons des produits écologiques, faisons des remarques aux gens qui jettent n'importe quoi dans la rue. J'évite de gaspiller l'énergie.
                                                                                                            Marie

Quand je vais en ville, et que je respire les gaz d'échappement, je me demande pourquoi les voitures électriques n'existent pas. On devrait jeter son papier de bonbon à la poubelle au lieu de le jeter par terre, on devrait acheter des vaporisateurs qui préservent la couche d'ozone.
                                                                                                            Céline

Adapted from *Okapi*, 1–15 janvier 1993

---

2. All three speakers mention the same anti-social action. Write down Henri's description of it (in French).

3. Find the French for:
   (a) the protection of the planet is vital
   (b) we collect glass and batteries to recycle them
   (c) we buy environmentally friendly products
   (d) I avoid wasting energy
   (e) exhaust fumes
   (f) aerosols which do not harm the ozone layer.

Check your answers in Chapter Eight.

4. Look at Céline's statements:
   '. . . on devrait jeter son papier de bonbon à la poubelle.'
   '. . . on devrait acheter des vaporisateurs qui préservent la couche d'ozone.'

   The verb used in both these statements is **devrait**, the conditional tense of 'devoir', and it usually is expressed in English by the word 'ought'. Using the vocabulary that you have collected in questions 2 and 3, and any other relevant vocabulary that you know, write four things that we **ought to do** to preserve the environment (**on devrait. . . nous devrions. . .**).

5. Now write a paragraph stating at least five things which there ought to be in your school. Use the conditional tense of devoir. (Note the phrase **il devrait y avoir** = there ought to be.)

   The aspects of school you might consider are: les devoirs, l'uniforme, les horaires, la discipline, les matières, les professeurs, la cantine and whatever else you can think of.

   Add reasons for the changes you would like to see, using the conjunctions 'parce que' and 'car' and use phrases such as 'Dans mon collège', 'en ce moment', 'je suis convaincu/sûr que'. For example: Dans mon collège, nous devrions avoir plus de sport, car en ce moment nous avons seulement une heure par semaine.
   Il devrait y avoir plus de choix à la cantine, parce que tout le monde n'aime pas. . .

   When you have finished, check your work in the following way; one thing at a time.
   - Check all plural nouns and adjectives to see that they have a plural ending (s or x).
   - Check all words for accents.
   - Check all genders: le, la, mon, ma etc.
   - Check all verb endings. Do they agree with their subjects?

   Copy any new vocabulary and useful structures into your collection.

TASK 6 ✍

Some young French people tell us about their relationships with their grandparents

---

Êtes-vous proches de vos grands-parents?

Je trouve mes grands-parents géniaux. Ils sont un peu d'une autre époque, ils ne pensent pas comme nous, ils n'ont pas les mêmes idées. Mais je me sens bien chez eux et à l'heure du café j'aime discuter et manger des petits gâteaux avec eux.   ***Mathias***

Moi, j'adore ma grand-mère. Nous nous racontons presque tous nos soucis. Je trouve merveilleux que deux personnes d'âges si différents s'entendent aussi bien.   ***Marie***

Je m'entends très bien avec mon grand-père. J'aime discuter avec lui des événements du monde, de toutes ces choses importantes, qu'il sait expliquer avec raison. Jamais je ne pourrais le trouver ennuyeux, je me sens toujours à l'aise avec lui.   ***Claude***

J'ai des grands-parents qui habitent assez loin de chez moi, ils ont neuf enfants et je ne sais combien de petits-enfants; mais ils ne s'intéressent pas à eux. Ce qui les intéresse surtout, c'est l'argent. Je suis triste qu'ils ne jouent pas leur rôle de grands-parents.   ***Catherine***

Adapted from *Okapi*, 15–31 mai 1993

---

1. Read what Mathias says and write down in French:
   (a) two ways in which he expresses his feelings about his grandparents;
   (b) three ways in which he comments on the difference between him and his grandparents;
   (c) two things that he likes doing with them.

2. Read what Marie says and write down in French:
   (a) how she feels about her grandmother;
   (b) what she and her grandmother do.

3. Read what Claude says and write down in French:
   (a) three ways in which he describes his feelings about his grandfather;
   (b) what he likes doing with him.

4. How does Catherine feel about her relationship with her grandparents?

   Check your answers in Chapter Eight.

5. Look at this phrase in Catherine's notes:
   'ils ne s'intéressent pas à eux' = they are not interested in them.
   You can adapt this phrase to fit many situations, but to do so correctly you must change not only
   the reflexive verb (ils ne s'intéressent pas), but also the pronoun eux which comes after à.
   Study the following:
   je m'intéresse au sport (in sport)
   nous nous intéressons à la musique (in music)
   il ne s'intéresse pas à moi (in me)
   tu t'intéresses à lui? (in him?)
   vous vous intéressez à elle/à Marie (in her/Mary)
   elles s'intéressent à nous (in us)

   Write down:
   (a) two things or people that you are interested in;
   (b) two things or people that a friend is interested in;
   (c) two things or people that your parents are interested in.

6. Now look at another phrase in Catherine's letter.
   'Ce qui les intéresse surtout, c'est l'argent' = what interests them above all is money.
   This is a very useful structure which you can adapt to suit many situations. Here are some
   examples:
   Ce qui m'intéresse surtout, c'est la lecture.
   Ce qui m'intéresse au collège, ce sont les maths.
   In these examples ce qui = **what** *is the subject — what interests me.*
   Now look at these examples:
   Ce que j'aime à la campagne, c'est le calme.
   Ce que je déteste en ville, c'est la pollution.
   In these examples ce que = **what** *is the object — what I like.*

   Write down five examples of this structure which you could usefully use in your writing.

7. Write a paragraph about your relationship with your parents. Use some of the vocabulary and
   structures above and use also some of the vocabulary from 'La guerre n'aura pas lieu' and
   'L'argent de poche' from the Credit Reading Section (Chapter Three) on pages 43–44 and 34.
   Begin with a general statement about your relationship, then state some areas where
   disputes may occur — or where difficult situations have been resolved, for example, l'argent,
   les sorties, la musique, la télé, les devoirs.
   When you have finished, check your work in the following way; one thing at a time
   • Check all plural nouns and adjectives to see that they have a plural ending (s or x).
   • Check all words for accents.
   • Check all genders: le, la, mon, ma etc.
   • Check all verb endings. Do they agree with their subjects?

   Add any new vocabulary and structures to your lists.

   *   *   *

We now come to the second section in this chapter, the section concerned with what you should do on the day of the exam itself. Before the exam you will have:

- worked your way through the exercises set out in this chapter;
- built up and learned lists of vocabulary, useful structures and joining phrases;
- tried out the tests set in the Credit Writing Paper in previous years;
- had quite a lot of practice in this exercise at school.

You will know what dictionary you have to use on the day of the test and will have made sure you can use it quickly and efficiently.

The time for the Credit Writing Paper has now been extended to one hour, so you should have plenty of time to write your views.

When you get your exam paper, read **quickly** through the short French passages and through the English questions which follow so that you know what the topic is and what aspects you are being asked to write about. The French is there to help you and it is quite in order for you to use some of the language contained in the various statements, but if you do, make sure of two things.

1. You should be able to work the phrase you want to use into the body of your own work. For example, suppose you read the French statement 'Quelquefois, ma famille m'énerve, ma petite sœur joue le rôle de la chouchoute, et mes parents les protecteurs bienveillants: je trouve souvent leurs réactions maladroites et enfantines. *Frédéric.*'

    You too might also want to say that your family gets on your nerves, so you can say something like 'Moi, je suis comme Frédéric. Ma famille m'énerve aussi.'

    However, it might not be your younger sister that you want to complain about, but your big brother, so you think of something he might do — and for which you already know the French — and write something like: 'Mon grand frère fait toujours beaucoup de bruit quand je veux faire mes devoirs.'

    (Do not waste your time by looking up 'chouchoute', 'bienveillants' or anything else in the French that you are not going to use.)

    You may then read the phrase: 'je trouve souvent leurs réactions maladroites et enfantines', and decide you want to use this structure, but you are talking about your mother and not both your parents, so you know that 'leurs = their' will not do. You realise that you have to adapt the phrase to something like 'je trouve ses réactions injustes/difficiles à comprendre'.

    (Again, do not bother to check on 'maladroites' and 'enfantines', unless they help you to express **your** views.)

2. Do not confine yourself to the French given on the exam paper. This would suggest that you do not have the language to say anything else and if you have prepared, as suggested, this will not be the case.

    Remember that you do not have to tell the truth! If you can, you may find it more satisfactory, but do not struggle to express ideas that you cannot put in simple French. Think of what you already know on the topic and use it.

    You will find that several points of view are expressed in the French passages, so you should be able to find something that is in sympathy with your own attitude on some of the aspects.

Now look at the English questions and decide how you are going to plan your work. It is worthwhile spending time thinking about this before you actually start writing. Notice that you do not need to write an answer to all the questions, but you should aim to cover several of them at least. Write down French phrases and structures which you think may be useful, then plan your essay as previously discussed, that is, think of a general introductory statement, develop this statement, writing a paragraph or a few sentences about each aspect before rounding off your essay with a suitable conclusion. You should know by this time how much you need to cover in your writing to write about 200 words. By all means, count how many words you have written if you have time and if this reassures you, but do not write any numbers on your exam paper. It suggests to the examiner that you are struggling.

Use your dictionary sensibly. Check any of the French words you think you need to know, but in the exam you should not use the English-French section except to check on spelling and genders, and on words you have forgotten. Beware of using completely new words — this very often leads to disaster!

Leave time at the end to check your work.

The following exercises are set out as they would be in the exam. Allow yourself one hour for each of them.

EXERCISE 1

Some young French people tell us about their lifestyle.

Êtes-vous en bonne forme?

Je fume depuis plus de trois ans maintenant et j'ai 16 ans. J'ai essayé de m'arrêter plusieurs fois, mais malheureusement je ne peux pas. Je trouve les sports ennuyeux, mais de temps en temps je fais du cyclisme à la campagne.   ***Marie-Hélène***

J'adore le sport! Il est la clé de tout mon équilibre: il me permet de m'amuser et de me détendre, tout en gardant la forme. Après un entraînement, je me sens d'attaque pour aborder mes devoirs et mes leçons. Je mange toujours équilibré, avec beaucoup de légumes et j'apprécie beaucoup les fruits.   ***Jean-Claude***

Moi, je ne fume pas. Deux fois par semaine je fais une heure de gymnastique. Au petit déjeuner je prends un café noir sans sucre et pour le déjeuner, une salade verte et du poisson. Au weekend, j'aime bien manger dans un restaurant avec mes amis.   ***Madeleine***

Moi, j'ai commencé à fumer quand j'avais 16 ans. C'était autorisé au lycée. Je n'aime pas le sport, je préfère rester chez moi à regarder la télévision, mais quelquefois je me promène en ville pour faire du lèche-vitrine.   ***Céline***

Je pense que pour un bon régime, il faut avant tout manger à des heures régulières, le petit déjeuner le matin, le déjeuner à midi et le dîner le soir. J'ai une grande passion, c'est le vélo. Quand je pars en vélo, c'est pour me libérer de tout: des soucis, du travail, de la ville.   ***Eric***

What about your lifestyle?
Does exercise play a large part in your life?
What is your attitude to sport?
Do you pay attention to what you eat — or do you think you ought to?
What do you think about school students smoking?
Are you content with your present lifestyle — or do you want to change something about it?

Write about 200 words in **French**. You may use a French dictionary.

EXERCISE 2

Some young French people talk about their attitude to their parents and friends.

En qui avez-vous confiance?

Je suis incapable de faire part de mes pensées à mes parents. Il y a un fossé entre nous, même si je les adore. J'irais beaucoup facilement me confier à ma meilleure amie. **Hélène**

Je pense que la plupart du temps nous n'avons pas assez confiance en nos parents pour leur confier nos problèmes. Nous avons peur qu'ils ne nous comprennent pas. Mais nous devrions essayer de nous approcher d'eux, car ils ont peut-être des soucis dont nous ne sommes pas au courant. **Laurent**

Pour moi, un ami, c'est quelqu'un qui ne se sent pas supérieur à toi. C'est quelqu'un qui aime faire les mêmes choses, écouter la même musique etc. On peut discuter sur n'importe quel sujet. **André**

Moi, j'ai des parents très compréhensifs: mes trois grands frères sont passés avant moi. Mais ma copine, aînée de famille, se dispute sans arrêt avec ses parents. Sa mère lui fait toujours la morale, et lorsqu'elle a commencé, elle ne peut plus s'arrêter. **Martine**

Mes parents ne comprennent rien: c'est comme s'ils n'étaient jamais passés par là! Ils ne prennent pas assez de temps pour nous écouter. C'est super d'avoir un ami sur qui on peut compter et à qui on peut parler de tout. **Françoise**

Who do you feel you can talk to?
Do you think your parents understand you?
Do you understand them?
Do you get on well with them or do you have arguments?
How do you feel when they give you advice?
What do you look for in a friend?
How important is it to you to have a close friend?

Write about 200 words in **French**. You may use a French dictionary.

EXERCISE 3

Jean-Louis tells us what he would do if he were Prime Minister.

Si j'étais Premier Ministre

Les réformes scolaires

J'essayerais d'améliorer la discipline dans nos lycées et d'établir de bons rapports entre élèves et profs.

J'aurais un emploi du temps moins chargé où il y aurait moins de cours et plus de sports mais je donnerais plus de devoirs aux élèves.

Je changerais les horaires dans les lycées et j'augmenterais le choix de matières.

La protection de l'environnement

J'essayerais de rendre tout le monde conscient de notre responsabilité en ce qui concerne l'environnement, par exemple la nécessité de protéger la couche d'ozone.

Je lutterais contre la pollution des eaux et de nos plages.

Je ne permettrais pas aux automobilistes de conduire en ville.

Je punirais ceux qui laisseraient tomber des papiers dans la rue.

Les problèmes sociaux

Je ferais de mon mieux pour réduire le chômage, en créant des emplois.

J'aimerais aider le tiers monde et je lutterais contre la faim et la pauvreté.

J'essayerais d'agir efficacement contre la drogue, surtout pour protéger les jeunes.

Je ferais une campagne anti-tabac et je ne permettrais pas qu'on fume au lycée.

What would you like to do if you were Prime Minister?

What changes would you introduce in schools? Do you agree with Jean-Louis — or are there other things you think are more important?

What would you do to help protect the environment? Do you think this is important?

What social problems would you like to tackle?

Would you like to be in a position of power?

Write about 200 words in **French**. You may use a French dictionary.

CHAPTER SEVEN
Hints for Reading Passages

Use this chapter only when you need extra help to answer a question.

▮▮ CHAPTER ONE   UNDERSTANDING FRENCH

Page 2   **Pique-niqueurs — campeurs**

Here are some of the words you may have found:

(a) which look like English. (Try saying them out loud if you are unsure of the meaning.)
pique-niqueurs
campeurs
attention
provoquer
incendie
proximité

(b) where ˆ= s: **forêt**

(c) where é = English es: **échapper**

(d) like other French words:
un réchaud. You know the adjective 'chaud' meaning 'hot'. Un réchaud is a noun. So it is a thing for making something hot.
emporter. You know 'porter' means both to wear and to carry. Only one will make sense here. *Em-* at the beginning of a word often has the sense of 'away from'.

Cigarettes and matches were **not** mentioned in the text. Your answers must be about the information which has been given. It is not a test of any background knowledge you may have, so check the text carefully before you guess answers. However, no answer means no marks, so if you are really stuck make an **intelligent** guess rather than leave an answer blank.

The key phrases are:
(a) **en forêt**
à proximité
(b) **Ramassez . . . pour . . .**
Laissez . . .

▮▮ CHAPTER TWO   GENERAL READING

Page 7   **Magazine**

Here are the some of the words to help you understand the passages.

A.   **estomac** — Take away the 'e' and say the word out loud. Of course it could still occur in almost all the passages so look at some other clues.
substances irritantes — Like English but we put the adjective before the noun.
stress — Taken from English into French.
un **remède** — This sounds almost like English.

B.   **bain**, **pieds**, **mains** — You will know these words from class work. You may normally associate 'bain' with one of the rooms in the house.

beauté — A noun ending in -é in French often ends in -y in English.
cuticules — A specialised word, but you will recognise the English equivalent if you read these kind of articles.

C. **J'ai 13 ans et une petite sœur de 5 ans. Mes parents sont séparés** — You will know these phrases from class work.
le même problème — Like English.

D. **jeune, sportive et regard d'un bleu intense** — You will know these phrases from class work. This is possibly the hardest passage to fit into a category. Leave it to the end to see what you are left with. Then read it over again to see if you have made a reasonable guess.

E. **omelette, crème, de crabe, paprika** — You may know these from class work or guess them from the English.
250 g, 200 g — These are obviously quantities and are a good clue to the general meaning.

F. **garde-robe** — A word beginning with 'g' in French sometimes begins with 'w' in English.
un twin-set et un short en flanelle — Like English. They may not refer to the same articles, but you do not need to know the exact meaning here.
(Burton, 269 F) — The proper name and price will also indicate which article this is.

Page 8   Drap de plage

Here are the key phrases you could have found in the text:
(a) pour **chiens** ou **chats**
(b) avec **capote* rabattable**
     pour qu(e) = in order that — indicates a reason, i.e. an answer to 'Why?'
     il ne **souffre** pas d'un **excès** de **chaleur**.

* capote: You may find two meanings of this word in the dictionary, but only one makes sense here. Look again at the illustration.

rabattable: You may not find the word in this form in the dictionary. You can see it is an adjective describing 'capote', but the closest you can find is the verb 'rabattre'. You will have to use your commonsense and think of a suitable adjective (here ending in ' -able' like the French word) or use a phrase (which can + verb).

Page 9   L'Étoile d'Argens and La Résidence du Campeur

Here are some of the main differences between the two campsites.

L'Étoile d'Argens	La Résidence du Campeur
À 2 km de la mer/Piscine	Accès direct à la plage par souterrain
Terrain de jeux	Jeux de plage
Pêche	Initiation à la plongée et
Canotage	à la pêche sous-marine
Pédalos	Tennis
Épicerie	Plats à emporter

Page 10   Avion disparu

(a) qui a **disparu** mardi soir
(b) Where the incident took place will affect the search as it is described as 'un secteur **montagneux et boisé**'
     You know the nouns 'la montagne' and 'le bois'. What would the adjectives be in English to describe the area?

Page 11   **Découvrez Paris. . .**

(a) and (b) These phrases all refer to time. Pick out the ones you need to answer the question.
   Toute l'**année**
   Une **heure** de croisière
   Départ toutes les trente **minutes**
   le **soir**
   De 9 **h** 30 à 22 **h** 30

(c) **PRIX**: Adultes, 30 F; Enfants de moins de 12 ans, 15 F
(d) DÉPART: Pont d'Iena, **rive gauche** — You will know 'gauche' meaning 'left' from practising
   directions. 'Rive' in French is not the river but what is beside it.
   au pied de la tour Eiffel. You will know 'pied' as part of the body (the part which **ped**estrians
   use!) — it is used here in the same way we use it in English.
(e) MÉTRO and BUS will be quite familiar to you. You will have to explain rather than translate
   RER.

Page 12   **Les cinés Gaumont**

(a) fix**ée** à 32 F — Remember the ending **-é(e)** may = the ending **-ed** in English.
(b) **depuis** le 16 novembre   **tous les jours**   **à n'importe quelle heure**

   You know the phrase 'tous les jours' and you recognise 'quelle heure'. You may not be familiar
with 'n'importe'. You see that the first part 'n' is a negative (like ne . . . pas — not or ne . . . jamais —
never) and you realise that the second part is from the verb 'importer'. When you look this up in
the dictionary you find the following entry:

> **importer[ēporte]** vt *(COMM)* to import; *(maladies, plantes)* to
> introduce//vi *(être important)* to matter; **il importe qu'il fasse** it is
> important that he should do; **peu m'importe** I don't mind; I don't
> care; **peu importe (que)** it doesn't matter (if); *voir aussi* **n'importe**

© Collins Gem French Dictionary 1991

   You ignore the meanings to do with *commerce, illnesses, plants* and *to be important* as they would not
make sense in the context of the cinema. But if you look at the very last entry, you will see the
instruction *voir aussi*. This tells you that there is a separate entry for **n'importe** in the dictionary.
Bearing in mind the offer is for '**tous** les jours' try to work out what 'n'importe' means as you look it
up under 'n'.
(c) pour les **moins** de 12 ans
(d) . . . faire **profiter** petits frères et petites sœurs.

Page 13   **Vacances avec les copains**

Here are the key phrases you should have found in the text:
(a) **chambres de six lits**   **sanitaires attenants**
(b) Grandes **salles** d'activités   **salle** de ping-pong   **salon** bibliothèque

   You will recognise that 'salles' and 'salon' refer to rooms. Can you work out what three rooms
are available?

(c) Un **brevet** de 50 m de natation est **nécessaire**. . .
(d) Any **two** of:
   mini-golf
   baignade — You know 'se baigner' and 'la salle de bain'.
   pêche — You are looking for an outdoor activity, not a fruit!
   découverte de la région — dé- at the beginning of a French word often = dis- at the beginning
   of an English one.
   campings

Page 14   **Serpents cachés**

(a) The first clue is that it took place **aux États-Unis** which you will know. To be more specific it was **à l'aéroport international de Los Angeles** which you can guess from English and the context.

(b) Did you work out what 'serpents' are? What was the man trying to do with them? Remember the key word **illégalement**.

(c) **Cachés** in the title tells you that the man was trying to hide the goods. But **how** was he trying to hide them?

Page 14   **Devinette**

Look at what the object can do, as well as the description.

Page 15   **Peanuts**

What had Marcy asked Father Christmas?

CHAPTER THREE   CREDIT READING

Page 32   **Hook**

la suite du livre
— you should recognise that 'suite' is related to 'suivre' which means to follow.
— try to think what we would say in English before looking up the dictionary.
— it is likely that the first English word given there is not the best for this context.
— choose the most appropriate meaning for this passage.

avocat
— tells you something about Peter Banning.
— you already know his full name, it's not his age or where he lives because you know the French for that, it's not about his family situation because that comes next.
— you conclude it must be something about his job.
— you realise that 'avocat' is very like the word 'advocate'. So you don't make a mistake in choosing a suitable meaning from your dictionary.

enlève les deux enfants
— you know that 'lever' means 'to lift'.
— 'en-' or 'em-' has the idea of movement away from (like emporter, emmener).
— you know that children are involved.
— you look at the meanings given in the dictionary and choose an appropriate one.

impressionnants
— you recognise that this word is related to 'impression', the same word as in English.
— you see that it is describing special effects.
— the trick here is that the ending -ant which is often equivalent to -ing does not help here.
— try to think of the form of the corresponding adjective in English as you look up the dictionary.

Page 34   **L'argent de poche**

Grammar note: Attendez qu'ils soient détendus
You know that **attendez** comes from the verb **attendre** which means to wait for. **Attendre que** means to wait **until**, and this structure is followed by the subjunctive form of the verb — **soient** has the same meaning as **sont**. (You meet another example of this tense in the article — the command form **soyez**.)

Vocabulary

criser — This has a connection with the French word **crise** (or, translated, 'crisis'). Read the phrase (Ce n'est) **Pas la peine de criser** along with the next piece of advice Expliquez-leur **calmement**. You can work out that the verb form 'criser' means something like (It's not worthwhile) making it into a crisis, making a big song and dance about it.

responsabiliser — You recognise the word **responsable** in this word. The ending -iser shows it is a verb meaning to make something — like the verb stabiliser to stabilise, to make stable. **Responsabiliser** then means to make responsible, aware of one's responsibilities. (Did you note the difference in spelling between the English and French?)

autonome — In small dictionaries you will find the word 'autonomous'. Do you know what that word means? You will know that **auto** means self — autonomous means living under your own laws, i.e. you are independent.

bisous — This is not given in the dictionary. Look for **bise** instead, and remember this has nothing to do with the north wind!

tendresse — You will find **tenderness** given in the dictionary, but the French use the word **tendresse** much more often than we use tenderness. A better word here would be affection.

Page 36   **'Tout à coup, la terre s'écroule'**

Prévenus, les parents de Nicolas sont là — Do you remember the advice given in the Tip for dictionary work? One thing you were asked to consider was the part of speech (noun, verb, adjective etc.) of the word you were checking on. This is very important here. **Prévenus** is a past participle, used as an adjective, describing Nicolas' parents. You therefore want to look up the infinitive of the verb, which is prévenir and means to warn, to inform. The sentence means that Nicolas' parents, who had been informed, are there. This is a very common structure in French, a very neat one which involves only a few words.
N.B. If you look up **prévenu** without giving it much thought, you will find a noun meaning defendant, accused. This can throw you right off course!

Epuisé, les lèvres violettes, Nicolas — This is a similar structure where the French do not need so many words as we do. **Epuisé** you probably know means exhausted, but to translate 'les lèvres violettes' we would have to add '**and with** purple lips'.

Page 38   **Il plonge dans le canal**

Il est des sauveteurs — **Il est** in this phrase is used instead of **il y a** for reasons of style. This is a more literary usage. You find it particularly in the phrase 'Il était une fois. . .' = 'Once upon a time there was...'. **Il existe** is also used in this way. Il est des sauveteurs = There are some rescuers.

celle d'autrui — Your dictionary will tell you, if you do not already know, that **celle** is the feminine form of **celui**. The noun it is standing for here is 'la vie' and the **d'** which follows it indicates possession, whose life it is, the life of other people. (Compare: ma bicyclette et celle de mon frère = my bicycle and my brother's.)

anonymes — **Anonyme** means anonymous. It is used here as a noun, to mean nameless people, nameless because they do not stay around to give their name after performing some heroic deed.

une fois leur geste accompli — This is another structure, similar to those in the text 'Tout à coup, la terre s'écroule', where the French does not need so many words as the English. We would say something like 'Once their gesture/act/deed has been made/done…'.

lui — This is used instead of il to give more emphasis. It is the subject of the verb 'a sauvé'.

CHAPTER EIGHT

Answer Guidelines with Advice and Notes

When you are checking your answers to a reading passage, you may well find that you have not used the same words as those given here. You will then have to decide whether your words express the **same idea** as those in this book and, if this is the case, you should give yourself credit for being correct.

In questions which call for an opinion, you may very well have written something quite different from what is in the book, and you should certainly not assume that you are wrong. If you justify any opinion by supporting it correctly with details from the text, it is very likely that you will get credit for this in the exam.

Although you will naturally want to see how many marks you have obtained for each text, so that you can keep a check on how you are progressing, this is really not so important as making sure that you now understand the passage and see where you went wrong, if indeed you did so. If you are unsure about any of the answers for the guided passages, look back at Chapter Seven to find the key phrases for each question.

CHAPTER ONE   UNDERSTANDING FRENCH

Page	Answer	Marks	Advice and Notes
2–3	**Pique-niqueurs — campeurs** (a) * In the forests (of Provence) * or nearby.	2	*In your actual exam paper the lines as well as the marks will indicate the number of points of information sought. The information in brackets is correct but not absolutely necessary for you to be awarded the points.*
	(b) * Pick up your litter * and take it away with you/take it home. * Leave the forest clean.	3	*The information after / is an alternative way of expressing the same point. You may have stated the same idea in other words.*

Notice how these answers would be marked:

Page	Answer	Marks	Advice and Notes
2–3	(a) In the forêts. * In the forests or near people.	0 1	*You have not shown you understand the French.* *You have given one correct and one wrong piece of information.*
	(b) * Pick up your litter * and take it home. * Leave the forest clean. Don't smoke.	2	*You have given all the information required for the answer. But you have also included extra details which are wrong. You may lose up to 1 point for doing this in any one question. This prevents people writing down all the reasons they can think of in the hope that some of them will be right!*

Page	Answer	Marks	Advice and Notes
2–3	Don't smoke and don't play with matches. Be careful.	0	*This information is not given in the passage.*
	Use a stove.	0	*You are told in the passage 'même un réchaud' — you are **not** allowed to light **even** a stove.*
	Do not light fires.	0	*This information is given in the wording of question (a).*

▌▌ CHAPTER TWO   GENERAL READING

Page	Answer	Marks	Advice and Notes
7	**Magazine** 1. Cookery. *E 2. Fashion. *F 3. Beauty. *B 4. Health. *A 5. Story. *D 6. Problem page. *C	6	
8	**Drap de plage...** (a) * dogs or cats (b) * the adjustable hood / the hood which can be folded down (c) * to protect the animal * from the heat / * so that the animal does not suffer * from (too much) heat	1 1 2	
9	**L'Etoile d'Argens/La Résidence du Campeur** I would prefer 'L'Étoile d'Argens' because * it has a swimming pool ***and** you can go fishing. (Or any combination of *sports ground; *canoeing; *pedalos; *grocer's shop) Or: I would prefer 'La Résidence du Campeur' * because it is nearer the beach ***and** you can learn deep-sea fishing. (Or any combination of *beach games; *diving; *tennis; *takeaway meals; *parasols; *guarded and lit at night)	2	*Here you will want to answer in sentences in order to make your meaning clear.* *Simply giving the name of the campsite does not fully answer the question. Nor does simply listing the features of one or both of the sites.* * *(Give **two** reasons.)*
10	**Avion disparu...** (a) * Tuesday evening (b) * Mountainous * and wooded area / * There are mountains and *woods (in the area)	1 2	

Page	Answer	Marks	Advice and Notes
11	**Les Bateaux Parisiens** (a) * Every 30 minutes. (b) * An hour (c) * 32 francs for adults * 15 francs (for children) under 12 (d) (At the 'Pont d'Iena') * on the left bank * at the foot of the Eiffel Tower (e) * By underground (to Trocadero and Bir Hakeim) * By fast train (to Champs-de-Mars) * By bus (number 42, 69 or 82)	1 1 2 2 3	*Not **in** 30 minutes.*
11	**Tip** (i) matin, après-midi, soir 5. morning, afternoon, evening (ii) durée, pendant 2. during (iii) (à partir) du, (jusqu') à 3. from, till (iv) tous les/toutes les 1. every (v) sauf 4. except		
12	**Les cinés Gaumont. . .** (a) * Reduced prices/Prices fixed at 32 F (b) * From the 16th November * every day * at any time (c) * Under 12s (d * Take younger brothers and sisters	1 3 1 1	
13	**Vacances avec les copains** (a) * rooms with 6 beds/6 bedded rooms * with adjoining bathrooms (b) * large activity rooms * table-tennis/ping-pong room * library (c) * a 50 metre * swimming certificate (d) Any **2** of: * mini-golf * swimming * fishing * exploring the district * camping	2 3 2 2	*'To be able to swim' would not really answer the question. You would have to have the certificate to prove your ability.* *You would not lose any points if you listed all five **correct** answers. But it would be wasting your time.*
14	**Serpents cachés** (a) * At Los Angeles international airport (in the United States) (b) * For trying to smuggle snakes (c) (He had 18 snakes) * wound round his biceps/arms * and ankles	1 1 2	

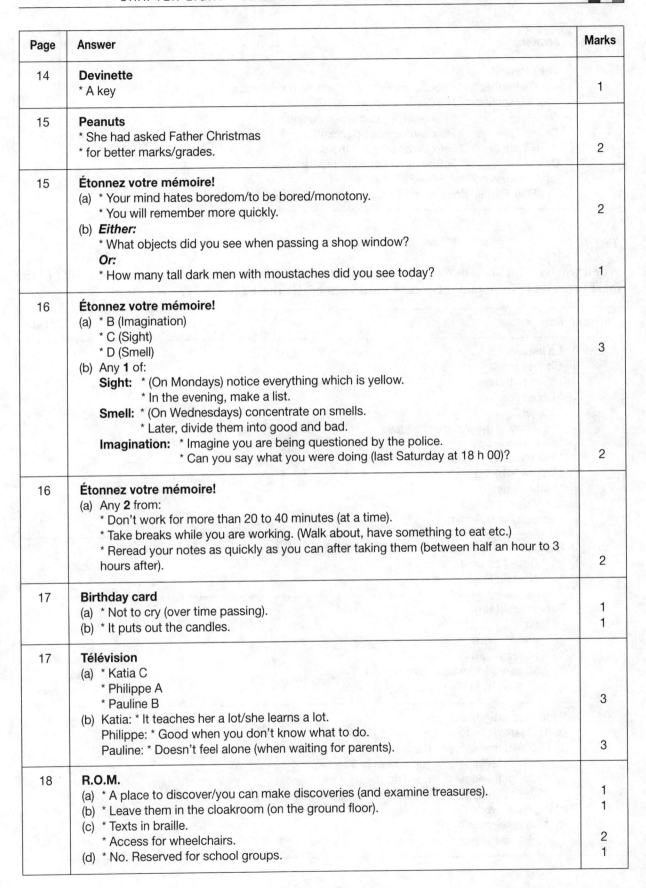

Page	Answer	Marks
14	**Devinette** * A key	1
15	**Peanuts** * She had asked Father Christmas * for better marks/grades.	2
15	**Étonnez votre mémoire!** (a) * Your mind hates boredom/to be bored/monotony. 　　* You will remember more quickly. (b) **Either:** 　　* What objects did you see when passing a shop window? 　　**Or:** 　　* How many tall dark men with moustaches did you see today?	2 1
16	**Étonnez votre mémoire!** (a) * B (Imagination) 　　* C (Sight) 　　* D (Smell) (b) Any **1** of: 　**Sight:**　* (On Mondays) notice everything which is yellow. 　　　　　　* In the evening, make a list. 　**Smell:**　* (On Wednesdays) concentrate on smells. 　　　　　　* Later, divide them into good and bad. 　**Imagination:**　* Imagine you are being questioned by the police. 　　　　　　* Can you say what you were doing (last Saturday at 18 h 00)?	3 2
16	**Étonnez votre mémoire!** (a) Any **2** from: 　* Don't work for more than 20 to 40 minutes (at a time). 　* Take breaks while you are working. (Walk about, have something to eat etc.) 　* Reread your notes as quickly as you can after taking them (between half an hour to 3 hours after).	2
17	**Birthday card** (a) * Not to cry (over time passing). (b) * It puts out the candles.	1 1
17	**Télévision** (a) * Katia C 　　* Philippe A 　　* Pauline B (b) Katia: * It teaches her a lot/she learns a lot. 　Philippe: * Good when you don't know what to do. 　Pauline: * Doesn't feel alone (when waiting for parents).	3 3
18	**R.O.M.** (a) * A place to discover/you can make discoveries (and examine treasures). (b) * Leave them in the cloakroom (on the ground floor). (c) * Texts in braille. 　　* Access for wheelchairs. (d) * No. Reserved for school groups.	1 1 2 1

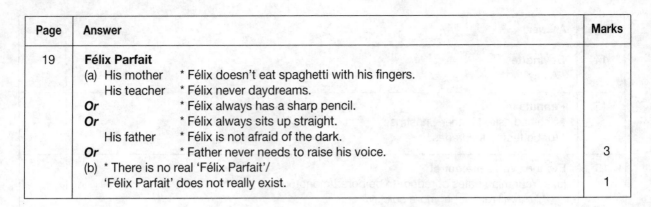

Page	Answer	Marks

19	**Félix Parfait**
	(a) His mother * Félix doesn't eat spaghetti with his fingers.
	      His teacher * Félix never daydreams.
	   Or * Félix always has a sharp pencil.
	   Or * Félix always sits up straight.
	      His father * Félix is not afraid of the dark.
	   Or * Father never needs to raise his voice.
		3

	(b) * There is no real 'Félix Parfait'/ 'Félix Parfait' does not really exist.	1

Test 1

When you have finished marking this test, total your marks out of 28. You must achieve 50% of the marks (over 14) to obtain a Grade 4, and 75% of the marks (over 21) for a Grade 3.

Page	Answer	Marks
20	**La liste. . .** Choose any **3** from the list: * (Her) birthday * Christmas * Easter * First day of the summer holidays * New Year's Day * Her name day/Saint's day * Mother's birthday * Father's birthday * First day of spring * First day of summer	3
20	**Exclusif** (a) * Books by post (b) * Nearest Post Office	1 1
21	**Service militaire** (a) * Girls	1
	(b) * Ireland * Luxembourg	2
	(c) * Military service lasts 10 months in Belgium * 25 months in the Greek navy.	2
21	**Vous êtes fatigués!** (a) B (Teenage health)	1

	(b) 50% of teenagers *feel tired
	   *25% of teenagers suffer from headaches
	    20% of teenagers *wake up frequently at night
	   *10% of teenagers regularly have nightmares.
		4

	(c) * School work	1
	(d) * Be patient * think of the next holidays	2

Page	Answer	Marks	Advice and Notes
22	**Luke Perry/Jason Priestley** Like Luke: *bored **or** *good at history, sciences and French **or** *hate maths Like Jason: *love school **or** *often first in the class **or** *rebellious.	1	*This will depend on your own attitude. Any **1** point from the given set of answers.*

22	**Salut! Concours**
	(a) * Record a song (on cassette)
	(b) * a photo of yourself
	  * the coupon
	  * the cassette
	(c) * come to Paris
	  * make a recording
	  * in a professional studio
	  * get 100 cassettes of your recording
	  * and photos of your day
		1
		
		3
		
		5
			Notice that this question is worth more marks than some of the previous ones. Did you check the whole paper first? Did you leave enough time for this question?

Test 2

When you have finished marking this test, total your marks out of 29. You must achieve 50% of the marks (over 15) to obtain a Grade 4, and 75% of the marks (over 22) for a Grade 3.

Page	Answer	Marks
23	**Météo** * B	1
24	**Parcs animaliers** Grandfather likes flowers *C *Rhododendrons, azaleas Mother wants the cheapest entry fee *C *Adults 28 F, Children 15 F Brother would prefer an amusement park *A *Free amusement park Sister interested in birds *B *More than 160 species of birds	2 2 2 2

Page	Answer	Marks	Advice and Notes
25	**Télévision** You will have chosen or rejected: *A — because it is a phone-in discussing problems *B — because it is about different sports *C — because it is a nature programme *D — because it is a 'soap'	2	*This will be your own choice, but the marks will be awarded for the reason for your answer. One point for explaining which one you like and one for explaining the one you don't like.*

26	**200 dollars**
	(a) * Manager(ess)/director
	  * of a small firm
	(b) * To clear up mystery
	  * about death of one of her employees
	  * which Sarah believes not to be accidental
		2
		
		3	

105

Page	Answer	Marks	Advice and Notes
26	**Gérard Jugnot** * Not (physically) very strong/muscular/brawny * Used humour like a (secret) weapon/ like a slap/his form of karate	2	
27	**Roméo** (a) * He has learned to dress himself/to put on his costume and sandals. (b) * He should have learned the seasons (first).	1 1	
27	**Marie** (a) * The mountains/a mountainous region (b) * Give the impression that * all French people live/the whole of France lives in towns (particularly Paris) * they think that those who live in the mountains * or the country * are not cultured/sophisticated (c) * In spite of their great culture * they are intolerant (towards people like her) (d) * Have an open mind	1 5 2 1	*Again, your timing is important as this question is worth more marks than the rest.*

CHAPTER THREE CREDIT READING

Page	Answer	Marks
29–31	**Batman 2** **Stage 2** Characters: Batman, The Penguin, Catwoman, Max Shreck Actors: Batman — Michael Keaton Penguin — Danny de Vito Catwoman — Michelle Pfeiffer Director: Tim Burton Plot: Penguin causing terror in Gotham City Type of film: Action, spectacular Comment: Suggests it should do better than first Batman film **Stage 3** — verbs in first section: envahissait, livrait imperfect/past tense — verbs in second section: laisse, est, sème present tense **Stage 5** (a) * 4 years ago (b) * The Penguin, * Catwoman, * Max Shreck (c) * To deal a fatal blow to the city and to Batman. (d) (1) * Very successful throughout the world * less so in France. (2) * It was a bit gloomy. (3) * Stayed closer to the comic strip. *Or* The first Batman film was *very successful throughout the world, *but less so in France, because *it was a bit gloomy. *and* * Yes, because this film is closer to the comic strip.	 1 3 1 2 1 1 3 1

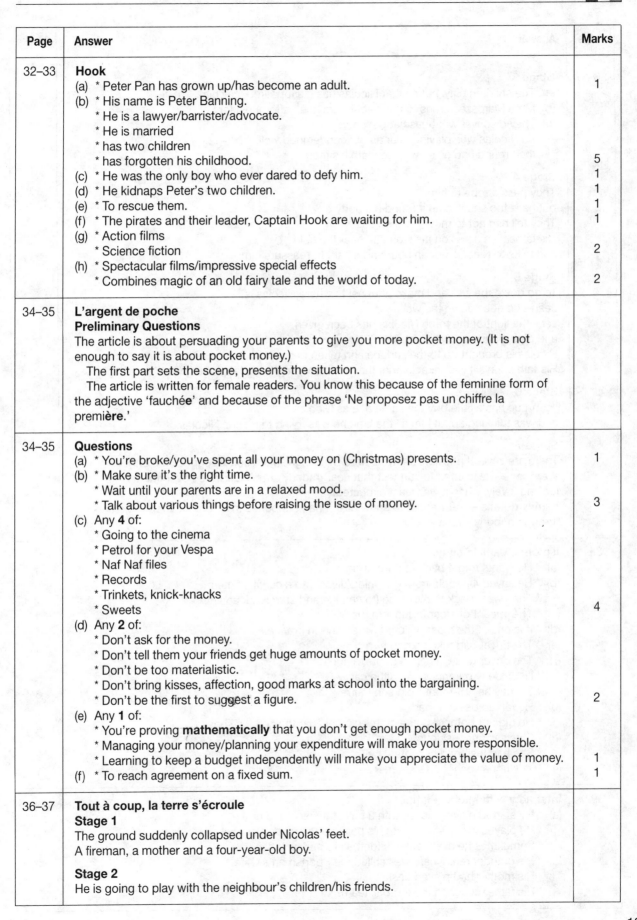

Page	Answer	Marks
32–33	**Hook** (a) * Peter Pan has grown up/has become an adult.	1

	(b) * His name is Peter Banning.
	    * He is a lawyer/barrister/advocate.
	    * He is married
	    * has two children
	    * has forgotten his childhood.
		5

	(c) * He was the only boy who ever dared to defy him.	1
	(d) * He kidnaps Peter's two children.	1
	(e) * To rescue them.	1
	(f) * The pirates and their leader, Captain Hook are waiting for him.	1
	(g) * Action films * Science fiction	2
	(h) * Spectacular films/impressive special effects * Combines magic of an old fairy tale and the world of today.	2

34–35	**L'argent de poche**
	Preliminary Questions
	The article is about persuading your parents to give you more pocket money. (It is not enough to say it is about pocket money.)
	    The first part sets the scene, presents the situation.
	    The article is written for female readers. You know this because of the feminine form of the adjective 'fauché**e**' and because of the phrase 'Ne proposez pas un chiffre la premi**ère**.'	

34–35	**Questions** (a) * You're broke/you've spent all your money on (Christmas) presents.	1

	(b) * Make sure it's the right time.
	    * Wait until your parents are in a relaxed mood.
	    * Talk about various things before raising the issue of money.
		3

	(c) Any **4** of:
	    * Going to the cinema
	    * Petrol for your Vespa
	    * Naf Naf files
	    * Records
	    * Trinkets, knick-knacks
	    * Sweets
		4

	(d) Any **2** of:
	    * Don't ask for the money.
	    * Don't tell them your friends get huge amounts of pocket money.
	    * Don't be too materialistic.
	    * Don't bring kisses, affection, good marks at school into the bargaining.
	    * Don't be the first to suggest a figure.
		2

	(e) Any **1** of:
	    * You're proving **mathematically** that you don't get enough pocket money.
	    * Managing your money/planning your expenditure will make you more responsible.
	    * Learning to keep a budget independently will make you appreciate the value of money.
		1

	(f) * To reach agreement on a fixed sum.	1
36–37	**Tout à coup, la terre s'écroule** **Stage 1** The ground suddenly collapsed under Nicolas' feet. A fireman, a mother and a four-year-old boy. **Stage 2** He is going to play with the neighbour's children/his friends.	

Page	Answer	Marks
36–37	**Stage 3** (a) The children play, notice that Nicolas has disappeared, call him. (b) Mme Maroszeck runs to the neighbours (the Lafforgues) for help. (c) They discover what has happened. As Nicolas was playing near an old condemned well, the ground had given way beneath his feet. **Stage 4** They pass a rope to him, but he is too small to tie it round his body. They tell him not to move/to keep still. His father lies down on his stomach near the hole and talks to Nicolas (for an hour and a half) to reassure him. **Stage 5** To go down the well and make a tunnel to where Nicolas is. Jean-Luc goes down the well, sees the light of the torch Nicolas has been given and digs a passage with a chisel. Nicolas is brought up to the surface and taken to hospital. His father says it is a miracle (that they were very frightened that they would lose him). **Stage 6** Jean-Luc has a little boy the same age as Nicolas and was thinking about him all the time he was trying to rescue Nicolas. **Stage 7** There are several possible answers here. Those given are some suggestions only. **Weather** — he wanted to suggest that near tragedy struck just when everything was looking lovely, when it was least expected. **Family details** — he wanted to show how it had happened in an ordinary family setting, through nobody's fault.	
38	**Il plonge dans le canal** (a) * He wants to get back to normal life. (b) * He saved 4 people from drowning/dived into a canal 4 times. * Then went back to his office (to change and start work again). (c) * The impact of a car falling into the water. (d) * It is one of the most polluted waterways in France. (e) * The driver had taken a bad turn. (f) * The driver was Catherine Scrite, a nurse. * Her elderly parents were in the car. * So was her 18-month-old son Pierre. (g) * He ran across the road. * He did not bother to take off his clothes/just took off his shoes. (h) * She was unconscious. * She had fastened her safety belt. (i) *He's not a very good swimmer.	1 2 1 1 1 3 2 2 1
39	**Interview with Michel Platini** (a) * He started playing about with a ball at the age of 5 or 6. * He played in the street (with his pals)/on the road to school. * Sometimes he even took his football to bed with him. (b) * His grandparents' café was called the Sportsman's Café. * His mother had played basketball. * His father coached the football team.	3 3

Page	Answer	Marks
39	(c) * His parents did not tick him off when he came home from football with torn trousers. * When he broke the neighbour's windows, his father did not tell him to stop playing. (d) * He scored (the) two (last) goals. (e) * A professional footballer's career lasts on average only 5 years. (f) * His career lasted 15 years.	2 1 1 1

40	**Les blues du businessman**
	(a) * At the top of a tower block
	    * that he is in control.
	(b) * He travels first class.
	(c) * He has lost his sense of humour.
	(d) * He is not doing what he would have liked to do.
	(e) Any **1** of:
	    * singer — * to be able to shout who he is
	    * author — * to be able to invent his own life
	    * actor — * to be someone different every day/to see himself handsome on a big screen
	    * artist — * to be able to say why he exists
	(f) * Material success does not bring happiness/
	The rat race makes you a prisoner/
	You lose your independence in business life etc.
		
		2
		1
		1
		1
		
		2
		
		1

41	**La folle histoire du skate**
	(a) * Two professional surfers (Mickey Munoz and Phil Edwards)
	    * could not train/practise
	    * in the absence of good waves.
	    * They made smaller models of their boards
	    * and put roller skate wheels on them.
	(b) * The rubber wheels were not suitable for tarmac/macadam/roads.
	(c) * New material/urethane and polyurethane/for the wheels.
	(d) * It became a camp-site.
	(e) * In the city/town.
	(f) * The fact that he asks the question shows he is doubtful/
	he's seen the popularity disappear before.
		
		5
		1
		1
		1
		1
		
		1

42	**Interview with Alexandra Tuttle**
	(a) * Journalist.
	(b) * She spent holidays/the month of July every year in Paris (and St Tropez).
	    * Her parents adore France/spend all their holidays in France.
	(c) * After finishing her higher education.
	(d) Choose any **3** from:
	    * Easier to live there.
	    * In Paris people look as though they are enjoying themselves/look healthy.
	    * Rhythm of life is less demanding in Paris/kinder to people.
	    * The apartment blocks are (only) six or seven storeys high.
	    * Extraordinary liveliness in the streets (despite an indifferent climate).
	(e) Choose any **3** from:
	    * Cafés always have lots of people in them.
	    * People stay there for hours.
	    * They talk about all sorts of things.
	    * The cafés have terraces (unlike New York).
	(f) *Formerly, Parisians did not decorate the streets and buildings at Christmas.
		1
		
		2
		1
		
		3
		
		3
		1

43	**La Guerre n'aura pas lieu — Part 1** (a) * (That you will be tempted by) drugs. * That you'll be in a car driven by someone who's had too much to drink.	 2

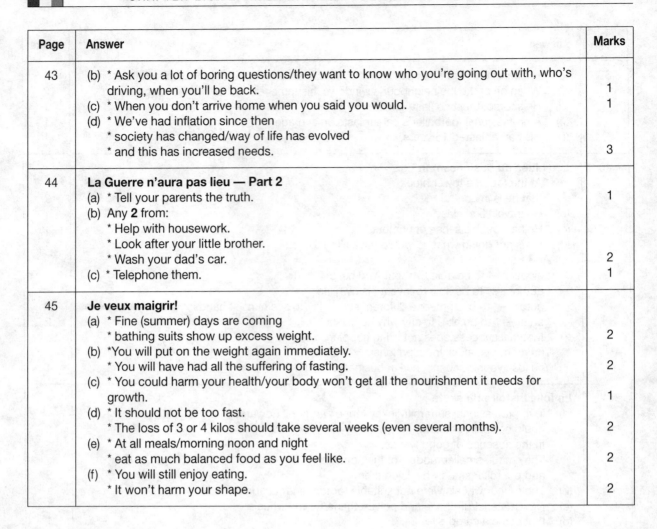

Page	Answer	Marks
43	(b) * Ask you a lot of boring questions/they want to know who you're going out with, who's driving, when you'll be back.	1
	(c) * When you don't arrive home when you said you would.	1
	(d) * We've had inflation since then	
	* society has changed/way of life has evolved	
	* and this has increased needs.	3
44	**La Guerre n'aura pas lieu — Part 2**	
	(a) * Tell your parents the truth.	1
	(b) Any **2** from:	
	* Help with housework.	
	* Look after your little brother.	
	* Wash your dad's car.	2
	(c) * Telephone them.	1
45	**Je veux maigrir!**	
	(a) * Fine (summer) days are coming	
	* bathing suits show up excess weight.	2
	(b) *You will put on the weight again immediately.	
	* You will have had all the suffering of fasting.	2
	(c) * You could harm your health/your body won't get all the nourishment it needs for growth.	1
	(d) * It should not be too fast.	
	* The loss of 3 or 4 kilos should take several weeks (even several months).	2
	(e) * At all meals/morning noon and night	
	* eat as much balanced food as you feel like.	2
	(f) * You will still enjoy eating.	
	* It won't harm your shape.	2

Test 1

When you have finished marking this test, total your marks out of 43. You must achieve 50% of the marks (over 22) to obtain a Grade 2, and 75% of the marks (over 33) for a Grade 1.

Page	Answer	Marks
46	**Ma vie est un roman**	
	(a) * Further back than our grandparents, only vague stories.	1
	(b) * Between those who want to leave a written record of their lives	
	* and those who can help them to do this.	2
	(c) * Tell the story of their life **orally**.	1
	(d) * The company sends someone to the author's house.	
	* Author has prepared what he/she wants to say.	
	* A recording is made (in three 1½ hour sessions).	
	* The tapes are transcribed and rewritten by professionals.	4
	(e) * So that the book remains open	
	* for (comments, photos) anything to be added.	2
	(f) * It takes time (4 to 5 months).	
	* It costs quite a lot (nearly 15000 francs).	2
	(g) * The telephone has replaced letters	
	* which could be kept/were a kind of written record.	2
	(h) * When the story of your life is written up, it reads like a novel.	1

Page	Answer	Marks
47	**La semaine de 4 jours** (a) * The school is opening a week early.	1
	(b) * All the pupils are there * except one (who will be back in a day or two).	2
	(c) * The introduction of the 4-day week * i.e. Mondays, Tuesdays, Thursdays and Fridays * no change in the hours (of the school day).	3
	(d) * Holidays are to be shortened by 10 days * One at Hallowe'en/All Saints * Two at Christmas, in February and at Easter * Summer holidays start three days later (on July 11th).	4
	(e) * They are well-behaved/orderly/ready to work.	1
	(f) * The beginners/those coming into the preparatory class * have visited their new school in June * the break with their parents is less painful.	3
	(g) * It is very long (3 hours in the afternoon, does not finish till 4.30 p.m.)	1
48	**Pour un monde à visage humain** (a) * Contact your local association for handicapped people * organise basketball matches with them.	2
	(b) * They might give you some pocket money.	1
	(c) * Write encouraging letters (through Amnesty International) * to a political prisoner (or a child).	2
	(d) * Give away clothes you don't wear any more * or toys you are tired of.	2
	(e) * By getting personally involved (with organisations such as les Restos du Cœur).	1
	(f) Any **2** of: * war * tyrannical political régimes * disease/illness.	2
	(g) * collection of glass from containers provided.	1
	(h) * He wants us all to make the world seem a kinder 'more human' place to less fortunate, suffering people.	1

Test 2

When you have finished marking this test, total your marks out of 42. You must achieve 50% of the marks (over 21) to obtain a Grade 2, and 75% of the marks (over 32) for a Grade 1.

Page	Answer	Marks
49	**Votre argent des vacances** (a) * Fill them well.	1
	(b) * Interesting activities are not free/you need money.	1
	(c) * Aurélien was broke during the holidays. * His friend worked in July. * Was able to have plenty of outings in August.	3
	(d) * That it was embarrassing not to be able to pay his way.	1
	(e) * He applied for a job in a bank (several months ago). * He has been taken on.	2

Page	Answer	Marks
50	**Interview with Antoine Prost** (a) * French schools are carrying out their function correctly/ French education has avoided changes made in other countries.	1
	(b) **Either** * In Sweden, hours of teaching Swedish have been reduced so that boys can learn how to sew. **Or** * In U.S.A. the teaching of foreign languages has practically been abandoned because languages were not required at university.	2
	(c) * The material/physical conditions pupils have to work in.	1
	(d) (i) * They are right to complain * about the dirty state * and the overcrowding of the premises. (ii) * Some have to be after 4 p.m. and during the lunch hour.	4
	(e) *Teacher cannot teach pupils to work if he does not have a good relationship.	1
	(f) * Discipline * Exam results	2
	(g) * No room for them in a full time-table	1
	(h) * Academic side/work/good behaviour	1
51	**Anna Chlumsky** (a) * Her father is a cook/chef. * Her mother has no profession. * They divorced early/before having any more children. * Father left (to run a restaurant in Paris). * Mother became Anna's agent.	5
	(b) * Japanese came (all the way) to Chicago * to get her to do some advertising.	2
	(c) * Singing, dancing, piano and clarinet.	1
	(d) * She learned the other actors' parts as well as her own.	1
	(e) * She loves school/is very studious/studies are very important to her.	1
	(f) * She has cultural interests. * She can talk about arithmetic just as well as about painting or cinema. * She is learning German/she knows some French through her father.	3
52	**Peut-être qu'en septembre** (a) * She is thinking of her lover * who lived in the house opposite * (nearly) a year ago * he left/closed the shutters.	4
	(b) * That he will come back in September.	1
	(c) * Her lover had played the guitar.	1
	(d) * He does not come back.	1
	(e) * No, she is now hoping he will come in December.	1

CHAPTER FIVE   GENERAL WRITING

Page 70

    (a) to catch a **train** — noun

        to **train** for a football match — verb

    (b) to **leave** the house — verb

        the **leaves** are green — noun

    (c) **last** week — adjective

        to **last** a long time — verb

    (d) to **long** for the holidays — verb

        to have **long** hair — adjective

Page 71

(a)	to catch a **train**	— **train** *m.*
	to **train** for a football match	— **s'entraîner**
(b)	to **leave** the house	— **quitter**
	the **leaves** are green	— for this you will have to look up the singular 'leaf' = **feuille** *f.*
(c)	**last** week	— **dernier(ère)**
	to **last** a long time	— **durer**
(d)	to **long** for the holidays	— **attendre avec impatience**
	to have **long** hair	— **long**

Page 73

le tour = turn, course, tour
la tour = tower
le livre = book
la livre = pound

Page 73

Ma ville se trouve dans **le** sud de l'Écosse.
La cathédrale et **les** musées sont très célèbres.
Mais moi, je préfère **le** stade et **la** piscine.

Page 75

faire la vaisselle	to do the washing up
faire une promenade	to go for a walk
faire le jardin	to do the garden
faire des courses	to go shopping
faire un pique-nique	to go for a picnic
faire les lits	to make the beds
faire du café	to make some coffee

Page 77

Comment t'appelles-tu?
Quel âge as-tu?
D'où viens-tu?
Tu es français? (français**e** for a female)
Tu as des frères ou des sœurs?
As-tu des animaux à la maison?

Page 77

(a) Où se trouve ton collège?
(b) Comment y vas-tu?
(c) Avec qui y vas-tu?
(d) A quelle heure les cours commencent-ils?
(e) Combien de leçons as-tu par jour?
(f) Quelle est ta matière préférée?
(g) Pourquoi l'aimes-tu?
(h) Qu'est-ce que tu fais le soir?

▮▮ CHAPTER SIX   CREDIT WRITING

Page 82

TASK 1 ✍

1. Le sport
2. L'équitation, la danse, le volleyball, l'athlétisme, le cross, le basket, le tennis, le football, le handball.

3. (a) pratiquer un sport
   (b) faire de la danse et du volleyball
   (c) faire du football et du handball
   (d) faire du basket et du tennis
   (e) faire de l'équitation et de l'athlétisme
4. Moi, je **fais** de l'athlétisme, et je **joue** au tennis avec mes amies. Mon frère **fait** du handball au collège et pendant les vacances nous **faisons** de l'équitation ensemble. Dans ma classe, les garçons **jouent** au football tous les mercredis et les filles **font** du volleyball. Et toi, qu'est-ce que tu **fais** comme sport? Tu **joues** au basket peut-être?

Page 84

TASK 2 ✍

1. Les jeux électroniques ou les jeux vidéo.
2. (a) je pense que
   (b) je crois que
   (c) je suis convaincu que; je suis sûr que.
3. Any 3 advantages from the following:
   — c'est un bon moyen de se divertir
   — les jeux électroniques sont utiles dans notre vie
   — ils nous occupent
   — ils peuvent distraire
   — certains jeux peuvent instruire les enfants
   — cela fait du bien d'en faire
   — cela détend les nerfs.

   Any 2 disadvantages from the following:
   — les jeux de combats pourraient conduire à la violence
   — ils peuvent nous faire mal
   — ils peuvent nous abîmer les yeux.
4. Florient — les jeux électroniques ne prennent pas une grande place dans ma vie.
   Lucile — les jeux électroniques prennent une place importante dans ma vie.
5. (a) C'est-à-dire   (b) quand même   (c) pour ma part.

Page 85

TASK 3 ✍

1. La campagne et la ville.
2. (a) Avantages de la campagne (any 3 of the following):
   — la campagne est calme
   — la campagne est moins polluée que la ville
   — la campagne est très verte
   — on respire mieux (à la campagne)
   — les gens sont moins froids
   — les gens sont moins agressifs
   — c'est silencieux
   — la campagne est un endroit agréable pour se balader à vélo (sans se faire renverser par une voiture).
   (b) Avantages de la ville (any 3 of the following):
   — il y a beaucoup de choses intéressantes à faire en ville
   — c'est pratique — le collège juste à côté
                     — les bus
   — on peut plus souvent sortir avec des amis, pratiquer des sports etc.
   — entre les magasins, le cinéma, la piscine, on ne s'ennuie jamais
   — on peut faire du lèche-vitrine, flâner dans les rues piétonnières, arpenter les avenues.
3. You have perhaps mentioned:
   j'aime la campagne
   la campagne, c'est le paradis sur terre

la campagne, c'est sympa
c'est génial
la ville est un endroit sympa
c'est vraiment génial.
4. (a) en ville
   (b) à la campagne
5. (a) pour moi   (b) quand même   (c) personnellement   (d) d'un autre côté
   (e) en un mot   (f) cependant   (g) en fait   (h) quant à (la ville)

Page 86

TASK 4 ✍

1. Elodie aimerait aller en Grèce.
   Claire aimerait aller en Inde ou au Népal.
   Paul aimerait aller en Australie.
   Stéphanie aimerait aller aux Etats-Unis.
   Anne aimerait aller au Bangladesh ou en Ethiopie.
2. (a) le pays où je voudrais vivre
   (b) serait la Grèce
   (c) ce serait en Inde ou au Népal
   (d) que j'irais
   (e) j'aimerais aller en Australie
   (f) je ferais un safari
   (g) je choisirais de partir aux Etats-Unis
   (h) mon voyage aurait un but humanitaire

Page 88

TASK 5 ✍

1. L'écologie
2. (Mes amis) jettent des ordures et des papiers par terre.
3. (a) la protection de la planète est vitale
   (b) on récupère le verre, les piles, pour les recycler
   (c) nous achetons des produits écologiques
   (d) j'évite de gaspiller l'énergie
   (e) les gaz d'échappement
   (f) des vaporisateurs qui préservent la couche d'ozone

Page 89

TASK 6 ✍

1. (a) Je trouve mes grands-parents géniaux.
       Je me sens bien chez eux.
   (b) Ils sont un peu d'une autre époque.
       Ils ne pensent pas comme nous.
       Ils n'ont pas les mêmes idées.
   (c) (J'aime) discuter.
       (J'aime) manger des petits gâteaux avec eux.
2. (a) J'adore ma grand-mère.
   (b) Nous nous racontons presque tous nos soucis.
3. (a) Je m'entends très bien avec mon grand-père.
       Jamais je ne pourrais le trouver ennuyeux.
       Je me sens toujours à l'aise avec lui.
   (b) J'aime discuter avec lui des événements du monde.
4. Triste.

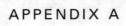

Choosing a Dictionary

We have stressed the importance of learning to use your dictionary before the Reading and Writing Tests. The best way to do this is to have your own dictionary so that you can make yourself familiar with it. The dictionary you choose now can last you for several years, particularly if you are going to continue learning French.

You will want to consider the following points when you go to buy one.

Purpose

You will not want to spend a great deal of money on something you may not need beyond this year. On the other hand, you do not want to find your first purchase is inadequate so that you have to replace it very soon. So, consider how much you want to invest in your dictionary.

Size

You will want one which is big enough for all your needs but where you can still find words easily. If you are going to take your own dictionary to school, remember to pick one which will not be too heavy to carry round all day.

When was the dictionary published and revised?

Does it have words which have only come into use fairly recently? If your parents still have the dictionaries they used at school, they may not contain words like *kilobyte* and *Aids*. You will want the most recently revised version to make sure the language is up to date.

Pronunciation of the words

Does it make clear the different ways you say *hôpital* and *hôtel, choix* and *joie?*

Are all the French words given for those which can have several meanings in translation?

Does the dictionary explain clearly which word is used and when? Try looking up *round* (a round of golf; round the corner; all round; to go round, etc.) and *would* (I would like to come; We would visit my grandmother in the summer; she wouldn't do it).

Print and layout

Is it easy to read?

Additional sections

Does the dictionary include, for example, verb tables, a list of abbreviations, business terms, useful phrases of time, lists of numbers and so on? Ask yourself how many of these you will find useful.

Quality of the paper and the binding

You may have to weigh up the cost of the dictionary with how well it is made, depending on how often you use it and how long you want it to last.

Progress Sheets

You may photocopy these Progress Sheets, and use them to help you think about and record your progress when you complete one of the tasks in this book or a class exercise. You can do this simply by ticking (√) those aspects with which you are happy, using a cross (x) with those which you are not and a question mark (?) for those in between. Then decide how you will improve your performance in the next task.

READING/LISTENING

General theme of text:

Approximate level of text: Foundation/General/Credit

Understanding

Without using a dictionary. . .
I understood the general sense of the text. ☐
I understood the details given in the text. ☐
I understood any implied meanings in the text. ☐

Answering

I was able to find the part of the text which was relevant to each question. ☐
I made good use of the dictionary, where necessary. ☐
I checked that I had answered each question as fully as necessary. ☐
I made good use of the time available. ☐

Next Steps: Areas To Be Revised/Improved

Useful new vocabulary to be learned	Exam techniques

■■ SPEAKING TASK

Kind of task:

General topic area:

Preparation

I had noted and learned suitable vocabulary. ☐
I had practised the situation in different ways/with different people. ☐

During The Task

I was relaxed and confident. ☐
I understood other speaker(s) easily. ☐
I was able to use a variety of expressions. ☐
I was able to speak at length. ☐
There were no awkward pauses. ☐
I maintained good pronunciation and intonation. ☐
I was accurate in using genders, verbs etc. ☐

Next Steps: Areas To Be Revised/Improved

Vocabulary	Grammar/Structures	Exam technique

▮▯ WRITING

Preparation

I read the question carefully and noted all the points to be covered. ☐
I knew or found out the vocabulary I needed. ☐
I organised my ideas before I started writing. ☐

Writing

I used varied/interesting/relevant language. ☐
I gave or asked for all relevant information. ☐
I checked:
    that all plural nouns and adjectives had a plural ending (s or x). ☐
    if any words needed accents. ☐
    that all nouns were used with the correct genders: le, la, mon, ma etc. ☐
    that all verbs had the correct endings. ☐
    that all verbs were in the correct tense. ☐
    I managed to express what I wanted to say in spite of errors in language. ☐

Next Steps: Areas To Be Improved/Revised

Grammar/Structures	Spelling	Exam technique

Revision Plan

1. This is a list of the topics prescribed by the Exam Board for the Speaking tasks. It is slightly longer than the one for Reading and Listening but includes the same areas. Notice that it covers only the kind of language you have been learning in class. So you would not, for example, be asked to express your views on world politics.

    You can use the list to organise your vocabulary notebook under topic headings to revise more easily for class tests and for the Standard Grade exam. Remember that it is also important to have a good command of the structures you will need for all the vocabulary areas — such as asking questions, expressing opinions and making suggestions.

    We have set out the table as a checklist so that you can use it to tick off each area each time you revise it.

Self			
Home			
Family/Daily routine			
School			
Work			
Leisure			
Holidays and travel			
Environment, places and facilities			
Food and drink			
Goods and services			
Accidents and emergencies			
Events (past, present, future)			
Concerns and ideas of adolescent and general interest			
Clothes and fashion			
People			
Personal belongings/ Pets/Money			
Places			

Immediate plans			
Time/Dates			
Weather			
Morale (happy, bored etc.)			
Physical state (hungry, ill etc.)			

2. You will need to recognise and use the present, perfect, imperfect and future tenses of at least the following verbs. Use this as a checklist each time you test yourself.

Regular -er verbs			
Regular -ir verbs			
Regular -re verbs			
être			
avoir			
aller			
venir			
faire			
dire			
voir			
mettre			
prendre (and comprendre)			
pouvoir			
vouloir			
devoir			
connaître			
savoir			
croire			
falloir			